T0199114

Born to Lead

from complacency to calling

SARA ESTEVEZ

WESTBOW
PRESS®
A DIVISION OF THOMAS NELSON
& ZONDERVAN

WestBow Press books may be ordered through booksellers or by contacting:

WestBow Press
A Division of Thomas Nelson & Zondervan
1663 Liberty Drive
Bloomington, IN 47403
www.westbowpress.com
1 (866) 928-1240

Cover art credit: Ruth Griggs

ISBN: 978-1-9736-6006-4 (sc)
ISBN: 978-1-9736-6007-1 (e)

Library of Congress Control Number: 2019904814

Print information available on the last page.

WestBow Press rev. date: 4/23/2019

Contents

Introduction

This bible study is a 10-week expository study through the book of Jeremiah.
This fascinating book gives us a glimpse into a time in history that
God used one man to intercede for a fallen nation.

We see the relationship between God and his chosen leader, God and his sinful people, God
and our enemies and God's chosen leader and the people he so desperately hopes for.

My prayer is that as you read the chapters of Jeremiah and use this study guide as a companion
to get through it you will experience our Lord in a new way, that you will learn things
about him you might not have known before and that you grow in intimacy with him.

Looking forward to the next 10 weeks together!

Sara

How to Get the Most Out of This Study

As you take this journey with Jeremiah the Holy Spirit will want to teach you new things. Guard your schedule so that life change can occur. During the next 10 weeks it is vital to make this study a priority so that you can grow in your faith. It is also important so that you can encourage your group members and they can encourage you. This book is a leadership manual. If you desire to be a more effective leader for Christ, a more effective follower of Christ and a more effective Christian this bible study is for you! Jeremiah teaches us what it means to be set apart in a fallen and broken world.

Each session is 5 chapters long. You can read a chapter a day and answer the questions in the study. Since it is 5 chapters long you have 5 days to complete but you can do them at your own pace. Discussion and teachings times will be held once a week.

The chapter to read will be located at the top of each page under the title and quote.
The symbol (v.1-3 e.g.) will prompt you to read that verse in the current chapter. If the verse is written in v.1-3 form it is assumed you are in Jeremiah and in the current chapter located at the top of the page.
All other books, chapters and verses to be read will be located throughout the study guide and will read, 'Read: John 3:16 e.g.'

The other two elements of personal application in the bible study:

1. Fighter verse: Pick a verse that stood out to you, one that spoke to you. Some will be filled in with a verse I picked out to pray over or use for memorization. When the area is blank fill it in with a verse of your choice from the current chapter.

2. Prayer: This is a place in the study that you get personal with God. Find a time and place to pray through what God is revealing to you for that day.

If you are looking for a bible study that helps you grow in Christ and know him more than you should commit your time accordingly. This is a 10-week bible study and requires bible-reading time daily. Life change happens when we commit to read and study the word daily.

May the Lord open your heart to all the truths He is about to teach you as you journey with Jeremiah through the broken Promised Land!

Chapter 1

"God is the God of 'right now.' He doesn't want you sitting around regretting yesterday. Nor does He want you wringing your hands and worrying about the future. He wants you focusing on what He is saying to you and putting in front of you ... right now." ~Priscilla Shirer

Read: verses 1-5

Jeremiah was young and unsure of his capabilities when he was called by God. It was the year 628 BC and the kings of Israel had grown complacent in their faith, disobedient, and evil. He ministered to God's people for more than 40 years. His journey is an example of how we are called into leadership, equipped for the journey, and used by God for His glory. As you read through the book of Jeremiah put yourself in Jeremiah's place. Hear the Word of the Lord and think of God's people the way God does. Let this book be an encouragement to you. God has work for you to do and he can't wait for you to get started!

1.   Read Psalm 139:13-16

How does it make you feel that God had a plan for you _before_ you even entered you mother's womb?

2.   What purpose do you think you have? List them?

3.   On a scale from 0-10 how confident do you feel about leading someone to God or closer to God? Explain.

|——————————————————————————————————————|
0   10
No Way!   That's Why I am Here

Verse 6

4.   What inadequacy did Jeremiah have concerning his calling?

Verse 7

5.   How did God respond to Him?

Verses 8-9

6. How did God promise to equip Jeremiah to lead?

Compare these great men of God and discover their inadequacies/insecurities.

	Inadequacy/Insecurity	God's Response
David 1 Sam. 17:12-15 &28		1 Sam. 16:1, 7
Gideon Judges 6:15		Judges 6:16
Moses Exodus 4:10		Exodus 4:11-12
ME		

7. Do you have any inadequacies that keep you from responding to God's calling in your life? What are they?

8. What the hindrances that keep you from responding to God's calling in your life?

Circle all that apply:
Fear   Anxiety   Laziness   Complacency   Busyness   Personality   Indifference
Other:_____

Verse 10

9. What mission did God give to Jeremiah? Fill in the chart with your answers.

1ˢᵗ Actions

- ☐ Tear down
- ☐
- ☐

Then Actions

- ☐ [Text]
- ☐
- ☐

During this training process to become a godly leader there will things in you that will be uprooted, torn down, destroyed, and overthrown; maybe it's old ideologies about God, misinterpretations about scripture, sin patterns in your life or complacency. Whatever the case may be you will also be built-up and planted, to prepare and pursue the mission God has hand-picked just for you!

10. After reading 1 Corinthians 1:26-29, how does it affect your view on your *ability* to lead?

Verses 9-16

11. How do these scriptures reveal the way we become prepared for our mission?

Verses 17-19

12. What commands and promises does the Lord give Jeremiah as he prepares to lead God's people?

Commands	Promises
1. "Get ready!"	I made you...a fortified city
2. "Stand up"	iron pillar
3.	
	fight against but....

13. Name a time when you allowed fear to keep you from serving God?

14. Is there a specific ministry you feel called to but doubt and worry keeps you from it?

Fighter Verse:

Prayer:
Lord Jesus, please open the eyes of my heart, I want to see you through these pages. I want you to reveal yourself to me through my study time. Don't let my age, my past, my profession or lack thereof be a qualifier to completing the job you have for me. Let me see my true purpose and be ready to fulfill it.

Chapter 2

Verses 1-3 *How easily we forget!*

After God rescued the Israelites from the grasp of Egypt's Pharaoh it was a love story God had always hoped for- a people who loved and served Him. But it wasn't long until complacency settled into their hearts and turned their attention away from the One True God. God is longing for His people to remember all He did for them.

Verses 2 & 4

1. Who is Jeremiah's audience?

2. Is this surprising that he is to speak to God's chosen people and not to those who didn't know God? Why?

Verses 2-3

3. What was Jeremiah to tell the kingdoms of Jerusalem?

4. Why is remembering the good times with the Lord so important?

5. Can you remember a time when you experienced God so close?

6. Does remembering help you keep close to Him when you feel far from Him?

7. What activities can you do to experience God's presence?

Read:
____ Duet. 17:18-20

8. How were the kings of Israel supposed to remember the words of the Lord?

Read:
____ 2 Timothy 3:16-17

9. Why is it good for us to read the Bible daily?

10. How can you ensure that you don't forget what He has done for you?

Verses 5

11. Why is the Lord angry with His people?

Look at the contrast at what Jerusalem *use* to be when they were one nation. Look for the adjectives in the verses.

V3. Israel was _____.

V.5b...became _____

12. What does this reveal about what sin does to our life?

13. What was Jerusalem to remember?

Verses 7-13

14. What were the charges against God's people?
    Focus on v. 13 (hint: there are 2)

Cistern: A well used in ancient times to store water. They were deep holes usually 15-20 feet deep. Their purpose was for either community use or private use. They were made of rock and were covered with stone.

15. If God is referred to as Living Water. What does the metaphor correlate between building a cistern and sin?

"Whatever a man depends upon whatever rules his mind, whatever governs his affections, whatever is the chief of his delights, is his god." Charles Spurgeon

16. List some modern-day idols in your life? List things that take your dependency away from God and things that take away your thirst and hunger for him? (hint: money, Pinterest, work etc.)

Verses 14-19

17. When we are overcome by the idols of this world what does God call us? (look for adjectives and that describe His people)

1.
2.
3.
4.
5.

18. How easy is it to replace God with any of these?

Verses 23-30

19. We learn in these verses that God has jealously. Is this a new concept for you? Have you heard this before? Does it surprise you to know that God feels jealously?

20. Read 3 of scriptures below and summarize God's reason for jealousy?

____Hosea 13:4-8

____Exodus 20:4-6

____Jeremiah 31:3

____Hosea 2:15

____Romans 5:8

21. Describe in your own words the reason for His jealousy.

22. Meditate on what this characteristic of God reveals about His love for you?

Journal your thoughts here:

When discovering God's jealously we must remember that His jealousy is never of us or anything we have but for us- for our love. There is nothing we possess that He can ever be jealous of. It is our love that he deeply desires. A jealousy that comes from a parent's heart for a child's love.

Fighter Verse:

Prayer:
Lord, help me see the everlasting love you have for me. Help me grasp it and hold on to my first love. For it was you that loved me first even when I was dead in my sins. Thank you for this truth and help me share it with others.

Chapter 3

Verses 1

   1. What relationship is God using as a comparison to the one He has with His people?

Verses 2-5

   2. What does God refer to His people as?

Verses 6-11

   3. As God is judging Judah's offense he makes a statement," Judah did not return to me with all her heart, but only in pretense." What do you think this means?

Refer to 1 Samuel 16:7, Hosea 6:6

   4. What does God desire most from us?

   5. In what ways can we love God in pretense but not with our whole heart?

Verses 12-13

   6. What does God promise if Israel returns and acknowledges her sin?

Read:
__1 John 1:9
__Romans 10:9
__Acts 3:19

   7. How do these verses affirm God's promises in Jeremiah?

Notice that true repentance examines the heart and requires a turning to God. If we are to live differently than we are to turn away from the thing that is opposing God. True Repentance causes true heart change!

Verses 14-15

8. What is the promise God makes to his people?

Verses 16-18

Fill in the blank boxes (on the New Covenant side) of God's prophecy of things to come.

The Past The Old Covenant	Priests (Num. 18:1,7)	The Ark of the Covenant (Ex.25:9,16,22)	Animal Sacrifices (Lev. 5:5-6)
The Future The New Covenant	(Hebrews 9:11-15)	(Hebrews 9:1-15)	(Hebrews 10:9-12)

9. How do these promises change religion?

10. How does the New Covenant give us complete access to God without a mediator, without rituals, without death?

11. What responsibility do you think you have to tell others about the hope you have in Jesus?

Verses 19-25

12. Can you name a few idols in your life that pull away from God's attention?

13. How can you be intentional about not allowing the idols in your life to distract you away from time with the Lord?

Fighter Verse:

Prayer:

Chapter 4

Verses 1-2

1. What repetition do you notice in these verses from the previous verses?

Verse 3

2. What does unplowed grounds mean? (Mark 4:12-17)

3. What does "sowing among thorns" mean? (Mark 4:18)

4. According to Hosea 10:12 what should we sow in our hearts?

Verse 4

5. What kind of repentance does God require of His people?

6. How can you change the next time you are tempted to half-heartedly apologize?

Half-hearted apologies are not apologies at all. At the root is pride and indifference.

Verses 5-7

7. What is Jeremiah warning the people about?

8. Where is disaster coming from?

9. How is the enemy described?

10. Who is described as a lion in 1 Peter 5:8?

Verse 8

11. What was one reason sackcloth was used?

Read:

____Nehemiah 9:1&2

____1 Chron. 21:16 (read all of 21 for context)

   12. What picture does this paint about what our response should be toward sin?

Verses 9-12

   13. What is Jeremiah's tone toward the Lord? What is his concern?
      (Refer to Jeremiah 14:13)

Verses 13-17

   14. Describe the power of the Lord.

Verses 18-26

   15. Who is speaking in these verses?

   16. How does he feel about his people? Write down descriptive words that point to his emotions.

   17. Reread verses 18 and 22.

   18. What actions led to these consequences?

God accused them of not knowing Him. They were Hebrews- they knew of Him, the stories passed down, the history told of Him long ago but they didn't intimately know Him. They had the written law and they had religion but they did not have fellowship with Him.

   19. How can you know of God and yet not intimately experience God?

   20. What is your relationship like with the Lord? Do you know of Him or do you have fellowship with Him?

Verses 27-31 *Business as usual when calamity hits!*

   21. What will the land be like once it is invaded by Babylon?

   22. Refer to verse 30. What will God's people be doing when calamity strikes?

   23. What is God's promise in verse 27?

A complacent life is one that has allowed culture normalcy or religiosity to settle in our hearts rather than fervency and passion for God. We trade in true meditation for mediocre prayer, relationship for religion, God's presence for people. While these things are not bad in and of themselves- they can be quick to lead us straight down the path of complacency. We cannot trade in true worship for the trappings of this world.

Complacency risks everything at the foot of pleasure and comfort. An intentional life requires one to keep the pulse on God's heartbeat. One must ask, "What makes His heart tick?" And the answer isn't a secret but a treasure trove waiting to be discovered.

How can you be intentional this week about not growing complacent towards God's will in your life? What steps can you take to intimately experience God's presence?

Fighter Verse:

Prayer:
Lord, help me feel your pulse. Keep me intentional about my walk with you. Keep me from complacency, that I may live for you and seek your presence.

Chapter 5

Verse 1

1. What were the conditions God was looking for in at least one person? (Refer also to Gen. 18:20-33)

2. What does this reveal about God's hope and will for His people?

Verses 2-5

3. What are the symptoms of a fallen nation?

-They feel no _____

-Refuse_____

-Hardened to Holy things

-Refuse to_____

4. Does this remind you of any nation in modern/present times? Why?

Verses 6-9

5. What are they being punished for (find 4-5 grievances)?

Verse 10

6. What does the Lord command to be done to Jerusalem?

Notice His "but" statement. What does this indicate about His discipline?
Read: (for further commentary)
____Prov.15:10
____ Romans 11:32
____Hebrews 12:6

7. Have you ever experienced the discipline of your heavenly Father? What was your response to it?

8. How would you describe the punishment of God to someone who thinks that God is only an angry God?

Verses 12-14

9. What power does God give Jeremiah because the people don't believe the words of the Almighty?

Verses 15-17

10. Notice the repetition of God's wrath and imminent destruction on His people.

Verses 18-19

11. Based on what you've read about God's discipline why do you think God won't destroy them completely?

Verses 20-21

12. What do you think it means to have eyes but not be able to see and ears but not be able to hear?

Verses 22-24

13. What claims does God make about himself? (Paraphrase)

14. Do you know anyone who knows the great power of the Lord and yet choses not follow? Include them in your prayer today.

Verse 25

15. What are the things that have made His people turn away?

Verses 26-31

16. God speaks of something other than idolatry they are guilty of, what is it?

17. According to James 1:27 what is true Christianity?

According to what you've read all week in what ways can you start living a more intentional life for Jesus?

Fighter Verse:

Prayer:

Lord, please give me eyes to see and ears to hear. I want to know your wondrous ways, your miraculous acts of creation. I pray that I not be complement in your calling. Give me a burden for your people and the lost, the ones who don't know your ways. Give me power to speak and words to say. Give me a heart for the poor and orphaned.

Chapter 6

Following the commands of Christ is not just about behavior. Behavior modification is not an end in itself in the New Testament. Transformation is about knowing the truth and the truth setting you free. If you'll follow Christ's commands, you'll follow Christ straight to your calling and you'll have developed the strength, grit, and stability along the way to handle it. ~Beth Moore

Verses 1-3
The bearer of bad news!

Jeremiah forewarns his people- the Benjamites, about the harm that is about to befall on them from the north.

Use the key below to decode verses 1-3.

North: Babylon
Shepherds: Heads of enemy nations
Daughter of Zion: Jerusalem

God uses the term 'shepherd ' to describe the enemy, a commonly used term to describe Himself, to show them the harshness of other shepherds. They refuse to be led by the One True Shepherd so He gives them over to other shepherds.

God's anger has risen against his beloved nation Israel because of their sinful hearts. Read Hosea 11 to grasp the relationship between God's just anger and His beloveds.

Verses 3-5

1. How will Jerusalem be punished for her sins?

Verses 6-7

2. What things is Jerusalem filled with? Why must they be punished?

Read:

____Exodus 19:5-6

3. Why are these sins so important to God?

Verse 8
Notice the repetitive warnings.

Repetition in the Hebrew language was used as a literary tool for emphasis when the point emphasized was very important. It is no wonder we see the warning of destruction over and over again in this book.

Repetition is meant to bonk us on the head until a lightbulb comes on.

4. What does this reveal about God's view on the urgency to turn away from sin?

5. What does it reveal about Jeremiah's love for his people that he would risk his popularity in getting this message out?

6. Do you think that the punishment will take His people by surprise or should they expect it?

Verses 9-10

7. Name 2 symptoms of a nation far from God?

-

-

8. Do you know anyone who is offended by the Word of God or someone who finds no pleasure in His words? (Pray for them today in your prayer time.)

Verses 11-12

9. Who will be affected by His wrath?

Sin has a negative effect on a lot more people than just ourselves. Sometimes its consequences are far more outreaching than we bargained for.

10. If you knew your actions would affect society to include your family and friends in a negative way would you change your course?

Our culture tells us that we should live to please ourselves. Circle the phrases that you've used most and the ones you believed most.

Follow your heart.   Live your own truth.   If it feels good than do it.
Life is relative.   Do what you want.   Go after your dreams.
Believe in yourself.

11. How might these statements lead us away from God's will for our lives?

Verse 13

12. Who is involved in offending the Lord?

Verse 14-15

13. What false security are the priests offering to God's people?

There is not a time when it would make sense for God to go against His word. Because God does not change, His word does not change. It is safe to say that if it is written in His word than we ought to obey it.

14. Has there been a time when you've taken your salvation for granted and walked away from God? What were the consequences?

15. Has there been a time when someone close to you was walking in sin but you chose to ignore it? Explain.

Read:
____Proverbs 24:24-25
____Galatians 6:1

Verse 16

16. What was the solution for Jerusalem?

Read:
____Psalm 119:9-16

According to the Psalm list ways you can walk on "ancient paths" and walk in the "good way?"
Verses 17-20

17. What has God done for or told to His people to avoid this tragedy?

Verse 19

18. According to the Lord why is He bringing judgment on His people?

19. According to Isaiah 1:3 (cross reference for Jeremiah 6:19) what is God's right to do this? What relationship does God use to describe HIs people?

Verses 21-30

20. What repetition do you notice in these verses as the previous verses (and chapters)?

21. How is Babylon described in this passage?

22. Who is speaking in these verses?

23. What emotion do you notice from the words being spoken?

Pay close attention to verse 27-30.

Read:
____Malachi 3:2

During the refining process metals undergo an intense amount of heat that completely melts the solid into a liquid in order to eliminate any trace metals and impurities to make it a pure metal. The only way to cure metals of impurities is to melt them, completely crushing and burning them into the refiners fire.

24. How does this metaphor describe the process in which God's people will have to undergo in order to experience heart change?

25. Have you ever been through the "refiner's fire"?

26. Is there something the Lord is asking you to be obedient to? Something he is calling you to or from? Is there anything in your life, an attitude, character trait, addiction, or habit that he wants to change in you?

Fighter Verse:

Prayer:
Lord I pray that you refine me during this time. I want to be pure and usable. Help me accept the things that seem unfair. Thank you for the hope that when you refine your people you do not destroy your people. Use my life to reflect your mercy, hope, justice, sovereignty and grace. Amen.

Chapter 7

Verses 1-2

1. What area and location did the Lord ask Jeremiah to deliver this declaration?

2. Why do you think God chose this location as relevant for His message?

Verses 3-6
Notice how God is always looking to be merciful to turn his wrath away from His children. He pleads with them saying, 'If you change your ways...I will let you live in this place." God is a good Father. He sets boundaries for us not for drudgery but for safety. He cannot allow disobedience in His house.

> Obedience is essential for the Christian life; we cannot call ourselves 'Christian'
> if we are not willing to obey. Obedience is a true mark of a follower of Jesus Christ.

Verses 4-7

3. God asked His people to 'reform' their ways. What is the cure for their weaknesses/sins?

Trust in deceptive words: Ephesians 5:6 _____
Hate/Violence: John 13:34 _____
Oppression for the weak: Luke 6:36 _____
Idolatry: Luke 10:27 _____

Read:
____Deuteronomy 10:17-19
____Zechariah 7:8-10.

4. What 3 people groups does God especially protect in these scriptures (notice there is no clauses in these verses?

    -

    -

    -

Based on your reading of Deuteronomy and Zachariah what do you discover about God's character that you need to *plant* in your life?

Verses 8-11

5. God further accuses the people of what sins?

1.
2.
3.
4.
5.

Read:
____Matt 23:1-5
____Matt.23:16-21
____Matt 23:25

6. What is the sum of all these scriptures?

A. God cares more about the condition of His people's heart
B. God cares more about spiritual rituals, outward acts of service and place they worship- religion.

Shiloh is first mentioned in Joshua 18:1. It was a place established where God could meet with His people and a place where they could meet with Him. It was in the city of Ephraim and home of the Ark of the Covenant and the Tabernacle.

Verses 12-15

7. What is God asking them to remember? Why do you suppose He is now asking them to remember something negative that happened to them and yet in previous chapters He was asking them to remember the good He had done for them?

Verse 16
When God refuses to listen

This also happens in Exodus 32:7-9 to Moses.

The Lord tells Moses to leave him alone so that His anger could burn against them. But Moses cried out for the people and God finally heard him because he loved him. (Exodus 32:11-14)
Is there someone in your life who is walking a path of disobedience? Have you cried out for them? Maybe you're the only one that God has crying out for that person. What would you ask God for them today?

Never undermine the purpose
God gives you in someone else's life.

Verses 17-19

8. Who is involved in idol worship?

9. How do you think it happened for once godly people to abandon (so drastically) God's truths and follow the ways of the world?

In the old story of Cain and Abel we learn that Cain sinned because he didn't offer the Lord a sacrifice that was favorable to Him (Gen. 4:5). We can assume that it might have been for unbelief or greed and pride. Did Cain not remember the God that walked and dwelt with his parents; the God that put them in the garden and the tough lesson his mother Eve had to learn after disobeying God's command. Or the honor of being part of the first family, did he forget about that? Did he forget that the sacrifice he was offering was to God Almighty, the Creator of the universe, the One who spoke face to face with his father?

Similarly, to Cain the Israelites keep forgetting the love and greatness of God that they quickly fall away. In Cain's story we see his many pitfalls:

disobedience, greed, unbelief, selfishness, deceit, rebellion, jealousy, anger, murder.

If you think these sins don't apply to you please take the perfection test and see how well you do.

I always obey God. T/F
I am never greedy. T/F
I always believe what God says in His Word and I never doubt it. T/F
I am never selfish. I never need 'ME' time or demand that my needs get met. T/F
I never rebel against God's will for my life. T/F
I never get jealous. T/F
I never sin in my anger. I never say mean things when I am angry nor do mean things. T/F
I have never hated anyone in my life before. T/F
If you answered false to any of these questions please read the following scripture.

Read:
____Mark 7:20-23
____Eph. 1:7

Pray over any of these areas that might cause you to stumble. If there is someone in your life you want to lead to the Lord pray for them as well.

"You will be accepted if you do what is right. But if you refuse to do what is right, then watch out! Sin is crouching at the door, eager to control you. But you must subdue it and be its master." Gen. 4:7 NLT

10. What is the key to *being accepted* and *mastering sin* according to Gen. 4:7?

11. How do you master sin your life?

Read:
___Col. 3:12-16
___1 Peter 2:1

12. Do you have a favorite verse that helps you combat temptation? Share with your group.

Verses 20-23

13. What is more important to God than sacrifice and worship?

Read:
___Hebrews 13:15

14. What type of sacrifice(s) pleases God?

Verses 24-26

15. How does God describe the condition of His people's heart?

Verses 27-29

16. Who does his rejection include?

Verses 30-34
God's fury worsens!

17. In verse 31 what specific practice are the people involved in?

18. Is it evident why God's fury would be spread upon the people?

19. What are some cultural norms that seem true and right or comfortable that women/ mothers may easily fall prey to in today's culture?

20. Can you think of ways fathers and mothers sacrifice their children to the culture of today?

21. What is God asking you to do differently in parenting, marriage, or as a child in your parent's home and how you view these roles?

22. In verse 34 what is the consequence for the people's complacency to culture?

Fighter Verse:

Obey me, and I will be your God and you will be my people. Walk in obedience to all I command you, that it may go well with you. Jeremiah 7:23

Prayer:

Chapter 8

Verses 1-3
We learn from Deuteronomy 28:26 that not being buried is a curse. Kings of ancient Israel were usually buried with some sort of riches in their tombs and amongst their ancestors and family members. Where and how a person was buried told a story of who the person was and how important he was while he was living. The worse thing for the living was to think they would not get a burial or lie out in the open.

Verses 4-6

1. What tone is God using in these verses? What draws you to that conclusion?

Verse 7

2. What comparison does God make here?

His people are unlike_____.
3. And who is the more obedient one?

4. And yet in Genesis 1:27, he says what of us?

Verses 8-9

5. Do you know any Christian preachers who have preached falsehoods? Any televangelists come to mind?

Verses 9-11
Warning for a horrific scene!

The Babylonians are coming and Israel lacks reverence and proper fear about things to come. The Lord is gracious to send Jeremiah to warn them that their backsliding will cost them greatly. He warns them that they will lose their possessions and worse, their wives. We may look at God as harsh for "giving" their wives over to other men but this is a warning of the harsh realities of war. It behooves Jerusalem to take heed. Do they? Time will tell. This is a picture of what sin does to our lives. It comes to destroy, ravish us and leave us for dead.

**The irony of sin: it seems right in the beginning
but regret creeps around the corner.**

When we grow complacent in our walk with Christ, when we choose to let our love die out, go astray or worse, deny Him, there are consequences. And yet He warns us about their coming, He takes His time in allowing us time to turn back to Him. He warns and He warns and He warns and if we're obedient and return to Him quickly we will miss the consequences of our actions.

Read:
____Psalm 81:12
____Romans 1:23-25

6. Why does God allow us to turn to the things that are not good for us, the very things that turn us away from Him?

Verse 12

7. What do the people lack?

Read:
____Psalm 38:18

8. How should we feel toward our sin?

Verse 13
When God takes away a blessing!

Read:
____Malachi 2:2
____Duet. 11:28

9. According to scripture when does God take away a blessing?

10. Have you seen this type of example play out in real life? Explain.

Verses 14-17

11. We see the enemy approaching and a people who are fearful and fleeing. Make a prediction. Will they escape the wrath of God?

Verses 18-22

12. Whose voice is speaking in these verses?

Verse 18

13. What name does Jeremiah use for the Lord?

14. What does this reveal about Jeremiah's relationship with God?

15. Can you name a specific time when God was your personal Comforter? Write and tell about your experience. Share this story with someone today.

16. What hope is revealed in His name?

17. What does this passage reveal about how Jeremiah feels towards God's people and his people alike?

18. How obedient was Jeremiah in delivering the "bad news" about the consequences of their sin?

19. How can you apply his example to your life?

Fighter Verse:

Prayer:
Lord I pray that I begin to take personal the sins of your people, this nation, and the lost. Equip me to deliver hard news so that I can then share the good news. Give me words to speak and a heart to feel the love you have for the lost.

Chapter 9

Verse 1

1. What sentiments are felt for the people?

Verses 1-6

2. Jeremiah and God have become one in mourning. Jeremiah shares the same sorrow as the Lord for the people. How is God asking you to become one in thought with Him over sin, the lost, the cultural norms that tear people away Him?

Verse 7

3. What truth do you learn about the purpose of God's punishment?

Verses 8-9

4. What "simple" sin is expressed here?

List the ways the tongue is described in these verses.

	Tongue	Outcome
James 3:6	fire, evil	corrupts the body
Prov.6:16-17	lying	
Psalm 31:18		

Verses 10-11

5. How can the attitude of God towards His people best be described according to these verses?

   A. A God who can't wait to see the destruction of the people for their sins
   B. A God who rejoices in the pain His people will feel
   C. A God who is deeply saddened by the consequences of sin on His people

Verses 12-16

6. Jeremiah is calling the people to judgment by telling them the effects of their sin.

What is their sin?

What are the effects?

Verses 17-22
A call for reformation

Verses 23-24

7. What should the strong, wise, and the rich boast in?

8. According to Psalm 49:16-20 why shouldn't anyone boast in the physical life they possess?

9. In 1 John 2:15 how is boasting of what we have described?

Verse 24

10. What godly characteristics can you begin or continue to *build* in your life?

Kindness and justice might seem like a contraction but because of God's perfect love and holiness He cannot allow His beloved children to be ravaged by their sin.

Verses 25-26

Circumcision to a Jew is an important rite of nationality and religion. It is a symbol of their eternal covenant with God, as was done in tradition with the patriarchs of their families.

Read:
____Ephesians 5:8
____1 John 2:15-17
____Galatians 5:22

11. How are we set apart from the world?

Fighter Verse:

Prayer:
Lord may I never fall away from your precepts. May I never give in to the culture to be pulled away from my first love. Impact my life that I may stay on the path of righteousness. Bless my children that their children will also walk in your ways.

Chapter 10

Verses 1-5

1. What repetition do you notice from previous chapters?

Verses 6-13

2. Who is speaking?

3. What does this reveal about Jeremiah's relationship with the Lord?

Verses 14-15

4. What names are used to describe idols in these verses?

Plug in a modern-day idol in the space below and use the adjectives to describe it.

_____ is senseless, without knowledge...

Rewrite V.16:

Verses 17-22

Notice again the repetition and urgency.

Verses 23-25

Notice Jeremiah's continual faithfulness to the Lord in prayer.

On a scale from 1--10 where are you in your prayer life. (10 being the utmost devoted to prayer, you'd consider that your spiritual gift.)

How is God asking you to *build* a more steadfast prayer life? What steps can you take to achieve it?

God shapes the world by prayer. The more praying there is in the world the better the world will be, the mightier the forces against evil. . .
~ E. M. Bounds

Each time you intercede, be quiet first and worship God in His glory. Think of what He can do, of how He delights to hear Christ, of your place in Christ, and expect great things. -
~ Andrew Murray

I realized that the deepest spiritual lessons are not learned by His letting us have our way in the end, but by His making us wait, bearing with us in love and patience until we are able to honestly pray what He taught His disciples to pray: Thy will be done."
~ Elizabeth Elliot

Fighter Verse:

Prayer:

Chapter 11

*It is not by personal holiness that a man shall enter heaven, but yet without
holiness shall no man see the Lord. It is not by good works that we are
justified, but if a man shall continue to live an ungodly life, his faith will not
justify him; for it is not the faith of God's elect; since that faith is wrought
by the Holy Spirit, and conforms men to the image of Christ.*
~C.H. Spurgeon

A covenant in ancient times was an agreement between two willing parties that set perimeters and expressed promises if the agreement was fulfilled.

In Hebrew, the word covenant is derived from the root word *bara* which means *to cut*. Usually the ceremony for a covenant involved the cutting of an animal, which validated the significance of the mutuality and finality of the agreement. The two parties would then be bound to their word and promise. It metaphorically represented what would happened it either party if they broke their promise. They took their promises seriously. Or did they?

Verses 1-5
A promise is a promise

1. What covenant did the Israelites break? How did they break the covenant?

2. Read: Record *who* the covenant is with and *what* is the purpose of the covenant.

____Gen. 6:17-18. Who_____What_____

____Gen.9:8-11. Who_____What_____

____Gen. 15:7-21Who_____What_____

Verse 6

3. What are the three commands in this verse?

Verses 7-17

4. Why do you think the covenant and God's laws are so important?

5. What was God's command and hope for His people through the Levitical law.

Fill in the blanks.

They are to make us _____(Leviticus 11:44)
But according to Romans 3:20 the law only made us _____ of _____(NIV).
We are powerless to be holy on our own merit. According to Galatians 3:10 the law is not based on
_____. That is why according to Colossians 1:22 we need _____ to present us
holy before God.

> *"When the Holy Spirit shows us our sinfulness, he does not do this to
> lead us to despair but to lead us to holiness. He does this by creating
> within us a hatred of our sins and a desire for holiness."*
> *Jerry Bridges ~Pursuit of Holiness*

6. Why do you think people of modern times cannot grasp the idea of a covenant and the significance of it?

7. Do you believe the covenants of the Old Testament are still important today? What is the significance?

Read:

____Hebrews 10:26-29

8. Does this confirm your answer or change your mind?

9. What do the covenants reveal about God's character?

Verses 18-23

10. Does God offer Jeremiah protection for his service to Him?

11. What was the punishment against the men seeking his life?

12. What comfort does this offer you, knowing that if God calls you to something he will protect you from you enemies?

13. Have you ever been fearful about talking about Jesus to others, not for the fear of losing your life but for embarrassment or because it was out of your "comfort zone"?

14. Is He asking you to step-out in faith in a certain area with a certain person?

15. What steps can you take towards obedience in this area?

Fighter Verse:

Prayer:

Chapter 12

Verses 1-12

1. Focus on Jeremiah words and complaint. Has there ever been a time when you felt like this?

2. Have you ever grown impatient with the things God has asked you to do especially when you don't see the fruit of your labor? Describe a time when you were worn out spiritually of waiting to see the outcome you had hoped for?

Compare these great men of faith and find the similarities in their attitudes and complaints. What were their *why* questions and what was/is God's answer, summarize?

	Why Questions		God's Answers
Jeremiah 12:1		Jeremiah 12:5	
Job 31:2-8 & Job 31:35		Job 38:4-7	
Psalm 10:1		Psalm 37:7 & Psalm 51:22	

Verse 5
Rewrite this in your own words.

3. What animal and action does God compare the difficulty of Jeremiah's calling?

4. In this any indication that God sometimes calls us to things that seem impossible?

5. Can you compare any area of ministry that may seem like keeping up with horses?

Circle the one that is the most challenging for you:

{Marriage}   {Motherhood}   {Church Ministry}   {People Ministry/Sharing Jesus}

6. Look ahead at Jeremiah 50:44 what promise do you see in this verse?

7. Is there a promise God wants you to grab a hold of in the midst of discouragement?

Verse 6

8. What does this reveal about Jeremiah's state of mind during this time of leading?

Verses 7-13

9. God shifts His focus from speaking to Jeremiah about his discouragement to "someone else" who is He now speaking about?

10. What does this reveal about the unity between Jeremiah and God? What do they have in common?

11. Do you feel like you are one with God in His attitude toward your callings.

> Pray that God would give you the same heart He has for the people you
> serve (your husband, children, church family, the world.)

Verses 14-17

12. What promises does the Lord have for Jerusalem's enemies? (Positive or Negative)

What does this reveal about God's character?
Check all that apply?

____Justice____ Good ____Mean

____Righteous Judge _____Compassionate

____Sovereign _____True to His word

____Faithful to His covenant____A God who is involved with humanity

____A God who hates humanity____A God who abandons humanity

____A God who even gives His enemies a chance

Fighter Verse:

If you have raced with men on foot and they have worn you out, how can you compete with horses? If you stumble in safe country, how will you manage in the thickets of the Jordon? Jer. 12:5

Prayer:

Lord help me not become overwhelmed with discouragement when faced with the mission you've given me. Help me be patient for your outcome. Help me love the people I serve and show them your love. Remind me that you love them more.

Chapter 13

Verses 1-11

1. What comparison is made in these verses between God's people and the linen belt?

2. What observations can you make from the significance of God giving this object lesson to Jeremiah?

3. What does it reveal about Jeremiah's character?

4. What did the illustration reveal about the relationship God's people once had with their Father?

Did you know:

From Jerusalem to the Perath (Euphrates) in current time it would take approximately 16 and a half hours one way. But in ancient times some theologians agree that it would have taken a week to travel a one-way journey.

The Lord called Jeremiah on this journey alone first so he could
then give the message God gave him to the people.

Before we lead others to God we must be the first to journey with
Him, we must be the first to change- the first to follow.

5. How long have you been walking with the Lord?

Verses 12-14 A Good Thing Goes to Waste!

6. What does this passage reveal about the heart of the prophets and priests?

Verse 15-16
Disaster always comes with a warning!

7. What sentiments does Jeremiah have for the people?

8. Are there any negative thoughts or attitudes towards others you need to *destroy* in order to better serve and point them to Christ?

Since we live by the Spirit, let us keep in step with the Spirit.
Galatians 5:25

9. Has God asked you to serve someone or minister to someone and the task seemed/seems impossible to stick with. Share this with your group.

10. Has there been anything this week that spiritually wore you out? Share this with your group so that they can pray for you.

Remember Jesus going to the cross, alone and abandoned, beaten, bruised, stabbed, tortured, and brutally mistreated. His flesh torn and ripped open, all while carrying a heavy, rugged, wooden cross, weighing approximately 80-100 pounds, with splinters embedding his shoulders and tearing into his skin. As the thorns pierced his brow and the precious sides of his face he was not given any sympathy by his accusers nor by his abusers. He was harassed by on-lookers who were there for the sport. He was shamed, for the garments he was wearing must have been torn, flesh must have been visible which left no privacy. Although the distance of the walk-up Calvary mountain is debatable it has been approximated to be about 650 yards in length (6.5 football fields long), nonetheless the journey was tortuous, long, and overwhelming; he did it alone for most of the journey, all the while thinking of you. He thought about the purpose of His life when His father sent Him, that he must fulfill His obedience to the One who sent Him for the hope that one day He would spend the rest of His eternal life with YOU. Let this picture motivate you to take the time for others, to pray for them, to serve them, to lead them to the One who died for them also.

Fighter Verse:

Prayer:

Chapter 14

Verses 1

1. What major crisis has afflicted the people?

2. What does this reveal about the gravity of sin?

> Sin is not outdated nor is it relative. The gravity of sin is still present in this
> generation as much as it was three thousand years ago. Times may change but
> people don't. Sin is sin no matter what generation you're from- the repercussions,
> still the same: separation from God, broken fellowship, a loss of clarity.

> The good thing: God is constant and we don't have to wonder if He's changed
> his mind on sin or not, or if He loves us or not. Our generation may say there
> are no absolutes and everyone is entitled to live how they want- but God wants
> more for you. He came to give us life abundantly not mediocrity. If we're living
> for the status of this life, we've settled for way less than He promised.

Verses 2-10

3. Who is crying out?

Verse 8

4. What do they refer to God as?

5. Yet in previous chapters what were they accused of?

6. Has there ever been a time when you were rebellious against God and only called out to
    Him in times of distress only to return to old habits?

7. How did that time affect your relationship with your Savior?

8. How does this behavior affect holiness?

Verse 10

9. Why do you think God will not help them during this time? After all, this is what God wanted, for them to acknowledge and repent and return.

Read:

_____1 Chronicles 28:9

____Deuteronomy 31:20-21 (focus on v. 21)

10. What does this reveal about God that man does not possess?

> He sees what we can't.
> He knows what we don't.
> Trusting that is the hardest thing we'll ever have to do.

11. If God already knew their hearts and minds and what they were disposed to why did he wait forty years in Jeremiah's time and seventy years in Babylonian captivity for His people to turn to Him?

12. What is it about God that makes Him wait so long for heartless, stubborn, evil people to come to Him?

Verses 10-13

Notice the conversation between God and Jeremiah.

Verse 13

13. What is Jeremiah pleading to God for?

14. Do you ever make excuses for not reading your bible? Going to church? Keeping in fellowship with other believers? Keeping in step with Godly behaviors?

> While these behaviors don't make you holy they are an outflow of holiness.
> As we pursue Godly living we pursue the things that are of Him. From
> holiness stems the desire for Godly things and Godly associations.

Verses 14-16

15. What is God's response to Him?

16. Why are the prophets and priests going to face judgment?

Read:

_____2 Timothy 4:3-4

17. What does this teach us about God's spirit against being "politically correct" and simply watering down the truth or worse, preaching what people want to hear rather than what is really true?

18. Have you accepted lies or misinterpretations about God's word? List them.

19. Have the last three weeks changed your mind on any of the ones listed?

20. Have ever "watered-down" the truth so you didn't "step" on anyone's toes? Explain.

Pray that you accept God's word, what is written, God-inspired and unchanged and know how to share it in truth and love.

Read:

____2 Timothy 4:5

21. What command is given to you here? Rewrite it.

22. What do you believe your calling is?

23. After taking your spiritual gifts survey on lifeway.com write them down in order below:

1.
2.
3.

24. Based on your spiritual gifts in what ways can they be utilized in your life right now where God has placed you? Whether you're in an office building, a church, or your own home.

Verses 17-18
Notice God's actions and His words for His people.

Verses 19-22

25. What is the tone of the people?

26. Based on your observations why is God *not* willing to answer their prayers and cries to stop the drought and famine?

According to 2 Timothy 2:24 how are we to treat those we serve and lead?
Write down things you'd like to improve on when you serve in your ministry areas.

Husband:

Children:

Church (other believers):

The Lost (Neighbors, family, friends, strangers, co-workers, social media friends, classmates):

> Holiness comes from pursuing the heart of God-
> adopting His will in place of your own.
> This comes with time with the Lord.
> Bringing others to holiness is
> letting them experience Christ in you.

Fighter Verse:

Prayer:

Chapter 15

Verses 1-3
God's anger continues against His people

Verse 4

    1. What reason does He have for his judgment?

Read:
____2 Kings 21:2

    2. What did King Hezekiah do?

Verse 5-9

    3. What term does your Bible use to refer to Jerusalem turning away from God?

    4. List some of God's punishment:

1.
2.
3.
4.
5.

"Let your daughter have first of all the book of Psalms for holiness of heart, and be instructed in the Proverbs of Solomon for her godly life." ~Jerome

Read the following verses and record other times the Lord allows disasters and/or trials on earth and in the personal lives of those he loves.

Verse	Purpose
Job 1:1-12	
Ezekiel 7:1-9	
Romans 11:32	
2 Timothy 3:12, Matt 5:10	
Job 42:5	

Answer according to your knowledge of God's character, true or false.

God is out of reach and unconcerned with humanity. T/F
God is desperate for our affection and obedience T/F
He is willing to allow pain in our lives to draw us closer to Him. T/F
He is jealous for our love and desires us to put Him first in our lives. T/F

Verse 10

5. Who is speaking in this verse?

Alas! is a deep cry of grief and sadness

Jeremiah voices deep regret and sorrow for his calling
to deliver God's message to the people.

Read:
____ Matt. 10:34
6. What do you think Jesus means in this passage? How does it explain the feelings Jeremiah has?

Verses 11-21
For intentional reading notice the conversation between Jeremiah and God.
Next to each passage spoken (in your bible) write the initial of the one speaking, G-God and J-Jeremiah.

7. How does this speak to you and what observations do you draw from this conversation between God and intercessor?

8. Think about your own conversations with the Lord. Remember when you pray or meditate to God it is not one-sided communication. He listens. He speaks. How will this impact your prayer life?

Verses 15-18

9. What are Jeremiah's concerns and complaints?

10. Look at the contrast between verse 16 and in 18. What happened?

Verse 19

11. How does God respond to Jeremiah, what is His tone?

12. What must he *not* do?

13. Have you ever been tempted to give into cultural norms and complacency because it seemed like everyone else was doing it? Or the struggle to be different is too great?

When the Christian life seems like an uphill battle remember
the charge you were given from the Lord:
"Be on your guard, stand firm in the faith; be courageous; be strong."
1 Corinthians 16:13

Don't give in! Don't give up!

14. What is the promises God gives Jeremiah once again to reassure him?

(There are 7)

15. Do you need to *plant* any of these in your heart today? Write them out.

16. Is there doubt, fear, unwillingness or weariness for your calling that you need to seek God for today?

17. Is the Lord calling you out of something that you need to consider? Perhaps a relationship, job, friendship, behavior, financial situation etc.

18. Have you taken the proper steps into obedience?

Ultimately God created us for holiness. Without it it's impossible to live out our purpose effectively. We are disposed to complacency- prone to wander but born for holiness.

Fighter Verse:

Prayer:

Chapter 16

"By perseverance the snail reached the ark."
~C.H. Spurgeon

Verse 1-4

1. Why does God command Jeremiah not marry in Judah?

Verses 5-9

2. What observations do you make about God's character based on this verse?

Verses 10-11

3. Does it surprise you that the people are asking, "What wrong have we done?"

   When sin becomes your culture after a while it is hard to believe it is wrong.
   It is hard to stop, hard to combat, and hard to resist.

Verse 12

4. How have God's children behaved more wickedly than their fathers?

Verse 13

5. Why do you think making the people leave the land is so significant to God? (Remember Jeremiah 16:5)

6. What truth do you learn about God through this passage?

Read:
____ Genesis 28:12-14
____ Romans 11: 25-29

7. Why is Israel so important to God?

8. Do you think Israel is still important to God today? Why?

9. What does Israel's significance to the Lord reveal about His promises to us?

Verse 14-15

10. What promises does God make to His people here?

Verse 16-21

11. What observations do you make about God in this passage?

God demonstrates his patience towards His people's heart by keeping His promises
to Israel. The nation of Israel is an illustration of God's unfailing promises to us.
God's love perseveres!

If God still stands for Israel what should your stand for Israel be?

For_____

Against_____

Fighter Verse:

Prayer:
Prepare my heart for the truths you want to teach me this week. Give me clarity when I don't understand and reveal your mysteries to me.

Chapter 17

Verse 1-2

1.   Where does sin wind up and what is the legacy it leaves?

Verse 3-6

2.   What repetition do you notice from chapter 16?

3.   What is the warning?

Read:

____Leviticus 18:1-5
____Leviticus 18:21

4.   What command did He give the Israelites as a nation for the first time?

Verses 7-8
Notice the qualities of a blessed man and compare them to the Proverbs 31 woman. Write them out on the side of the verse.

Jeremiah	Blessed Man	Proverbs	*Proverbs 31 Woman*
17:7	Trusts in the Lord	31:30	
17:8	Well watered	31:11	
17:8	Well planted	31:25 &2 6	
17:8	No worries	31:21	
17:8	Fruitful	31:13-20,22,24,27	

5.   What attributes do you want to *plant* in your life based on these two godly models?

Verse 9
6.   After reading this verse what do you think about the saying, "Just follow your heart?"

Verse 10
Don't Just Talk the Talk but Walk the Walk!

Read:
____Ephesians 4:17-32
____Ephesians 5:1-13

Focus on Eph. 5:3.
Put a check next to the ones you need prayer for. Focus on praying over these for the reminder of the study. Circle the ones that God has delivered you from and celebrate those milestones.

Negative	Positive
Sexual Immorality	Sexually Pure
Impurity	Pure Conscience
Greed	Generous
Obscenities	Wholesome talking
Coarse Jesting	Kind and Truthful Words

The Christian life is not about a label, a title, or demographics; it's a journey with the One True God who walks in front of us. We are called to keep in step with Him. It isn't just about what we say, it's what we do, what we think, how we live and how we love.

"Finally, brothers, whatever is true, whatever is honorable, whatever is just, whatever is pure, whatever is lovely, whatever is commendable, if there is any excellence, if there is anything worthy of praise, think about these things."
~Philippians 4:8

Verse 11

7. Which characteristics would like you to start praying about in your own life?

Verses 12-14

8. What truths about God's character are revealed in the passage?

Verses 15-18

9. Describe Jeremiah. How can you imitate him?

Verses 19-27

10. Why is keeping the Sabbath so important to the Lord?

We hustle and toil on Monday. We strain and toil on Tuesday. We rush and toil on Wednesday. We cram and toil on Tuesday. We celebrate and toil on Friday. We get up and go again on Saturday. We toil in our minds and worry about Monday on Sunday. It's no wonder we are all too tired, too busy, too concerned with toiling to tend to relationships, for realness with the people next door, too busy for hospitality or the dreaded phone call to say "hi." When do we settle? When do we quiet our souls?

11. Do you agree with the statement above?

12. How does this apply to you?

13. How do you practice the Sabbath? What are your Sunday habits?

Read:

____Exodus 16:23

____Exodus 16:29-30

____Exodus 20:11

14. Why was the Sabbath created?

Better is a handful of quietness than two hands full of toil and a striving after wind. Ecclesiastes 4:6 ESV

15. Are there activities that hinder you/your family from experiencing the Sabbath? Explain.

16. Would your life be dramatically different if you ceased to strive, strain, stress, or toil on Sunday?

17. Make a list of activities that hinder you from finding rest on Sunday, pray over it and ask for faith in this area.

"Rest is an important part of a healthy lifestyle for all ages. It rejuvenates your body and mind, regulates your mood, and is linked to learning and memory function. On the other hand, not getting enough rest can negatively affect your mood, immune system, memory, and stress level." ~ UW Carelink, University of Washington

Rest is both a physical and spiritual necessity created to rejuvenate you and to bring you closer to your Creator. It's a day for reflection on praises of the week. What's He's done for you, delivered you from, helped you accomplish. It's a day to enjoy Him.

Remember that the Sabbath was not created only for physical rest but it's what sets us apart from the world. While the world keeps going and toiling; we stop, give thanks to our God and rest in His goodness and faithfulness. The Sabbath is not just a religious practice it should be a spiritual experience you accept because the God who created the Universe calls you to.

"It is time for us to breathe and build margin into our lives for God. Sabbath was intended as a gift, and it is still a gift to us today. If you are weary, worn out, and exhausted the concept of Sabbath will change your life." ~ Priscilla Shirer

Fighter Verse:

Prayer: Lord, help slow down and enjoy you. Amen

Chapter 18

Verses 1-2

1. What is the location Jeremiah is to deliver God's message?

Verses 3-6

2. What relationship is depicted to illustrated God and His people?

God as _____

Israel as _____

3. Do you see yourself as clay? If so, are you hardened clay or moldable clay?

Read:
____ Prov. 2:3-5
____ Prov. 9:9

A servant of the Lord must not quarrel but must be kind to everyone, be able to teach, and be patient with difficult people. 2 Timothy 2:24 (NLV)

4. What do these scriptures suggest about the attitude we should have about being teachable and moldable?

5. How can your perseverance get you through times when God is trying to mold you into something better?

Verses 7-10

6. What important truths do you learn about God in these verses?

Verses 11-12

7. How does God prepare Jeremiah for the response of the people?

Verses 13-17

Even nature obeys God's ways and yet His own children rebel against the purpose of their existence-to bring God glory-to live for God-to be different!

Lebanon: "whiteness"

Did you know:

Lebanon's geographic region is mostly hilly and mountainous and the mountain peaks usually remain snowcapped throughout the year.

Verses 18-23

8. What is Jeremiah's concern and request?

9. Can you relate to him? Has there been a time when you've wanted to take vengeance into your own hands? Explain.

Read:
____ Romans 12:17-21
____ Psalm 94:23

10. Based on these verses how can we overcome the desire to take vengeance into our own hands?

11. How can you persevere through times of conflict with other believers or difficult people?

Look at the perfect example of perseverance and dwell upon it.

Read:
_____ Luke 22:42

12. What is the first step you take when you need a boost in your walk, in your calling- your Christian life?

Fighter Verse:

Prayer:

Chapter 19

Verses 1-3

1. What are the objects that Jeremiah is to take with him when he speaks to the people?

2. Who is his audience?

3. What is the location?

Did you know:

Valley Ben Hinnon *("Ghenna")* is the outer southern boundary of Jerusalem (Josua 15:8), was referred to as *hell* and the Valley of Slaughter by the Lord.

Verses 4-6

4. What had they used that location for?

Verses 7-9
Reader discretion advised!

5. What was God's response to the evil the people had committed?

Think about Jeremiah's commitment and perseverance for God's people who had committed such atrocities in the name of a false religion and false god. He was determined to point them to God no matter who followed him, no matter how they treated him, no matter what sin they committed, and no matter the physical stress put on his body. He loved God so much he was willing to take the call to lead others to God.

(Fill in the blanks):
He gives us a **Responsibility** to _____ them. (Deut. 6:7)

God gives them as a **Reward** to _____ (Psalm 17:6)

He **Relishes** their _____ (Matt. 19:14)

He gives **Revelations** through their _____ (Psalm 8:2)

He commands **Refuge** for them. (Mark 9:42)

He uses children to **Reflect** the relationship between us and _____ (Ro. 8:16)

v. 10-15

6. What is the object lesson {**punishment**} for the people?

7. How does he reference the Potter and the clay?

8. What is the **purpose** of this punishment?

Read:
____Lamentations 2:11-12
____Lamentations 3:5
____Lamentations 5:2-5

9. What **process** must the people go through in order to draw closer to the Lord?

10. Do you think that the parents, after watching their children die of hunger, had any remorse for the acts they committed against them in Jerusalem?

11. Do you think their hearts changed toward their children after this experience?

12. What was the cost of this lesson?

Read:
___Lamentations 3:31-33

13. What is the **promise** the people had to hold on to during the times of trials in Babylon?

Read:
____Lamentations 3:37-42

14. What should our response be toward our own sin?

Remember that God doesn't cause the young and innocent to die. The hands and consequences of evil people do. God is always there to make right a wrong no matter how long it takes weather we see it or not. This reveals how much He loves sinners.

15. Does it reveal God's rationale as He knows eternal peace and glory is promised to the innocent but the guilty must be separated from Him forever?

Read:

____ John 3:16-17

16. What does this reveal about the God of Christianity?

17. According to verse 17 does he come to condemn or to save? How does this differ from a worldview that says God is an angry God waiting to judge us and condemn us.

18. How can you defend God in words from this point of view? Think about all you've learned so far.

19. How does this defy the "fire and brim stone" theology?

Fighter Verse:

Prayer:

Lord help me not take for granted the innocent blood of my Savior. Help me grasp the depth of your love for me. Give me the heart to love you in ways that push me into action for the gospel.

Chapter 20

Verses 1-2

1. Who was the officer spoken of in these verses?

2. What did he have done to Jeremiah?

Did you know:
Pashhur was the son of a Levite Priest (1 Chron. 24:6-14). The Levites were from the clan of Levi (3rd son of Jacob and Leah). They were considered to be set apart due to their spiritual obligations and responsibilities in the temple.

> This fact MAKES A STATEMENT that no matter our spiritual legacies and heritage we still have a *choice* to follow or not follow God. We must not take for granted our spiritual legacy nor except any false assurance that may come with the title of "Christian." Christianity is not a religion. It is not a set of rules that saves us from hell. Let us not deceive ourselves, like Pashhur did. We will not escape God's judgment simply because we have a religious background, grew up in church, attend bible study, have been baptized or call ourselves Christian.

3. Think back to the time you accepted Christ in your life. How has your life changed from who you were to who you are now? Share with the group.

4. If you were raised in the church by godly parents at what point in your life did you make Christianity your own?

Verses 3-6

5. What is Pashhur's punishment for the acts he committed under his legal office of the Lord?

> Pashhur: *freedom* (prosperity everywhere)
> Magor-MIssabib: *"terror on every side"*

> Often, the Lord changes the names of His people in the bible after experiencing total transformation- from the old to the new. Often their

names get changed to signify their life change in Christ. Unfortunately for Pashhur his name goes from good to bad- from freedom to terror.

6. If the Lord changed the meaning of your name what would He have changed it to after you were saved?

Verses 7-8

7. Notice Jeremiah's feelings. Do you notice a change in attitude towards the Lord and his calling?

Verse 9

8. What does he compare the words of the Lord to?

Plot your spiritual state at present on the scale.

0——10

Cold as ice   Lukewarm   In flames!

9. If you did not mark 10, what is keeping you from experiencing God in this way?

Read:
____Luke 24:31-32 (Speaking of Jesus)

10. When was the "burning" placed in the two apostles' hearts?

11. Name an instance in your life when God placed a "fire" in your heart for someone or something that you couldn't contain it?

Verse 10
Notice the hardships and trials Jeremiah faces.

Verses 11-13

12. What hope do we have in our God when things seem hopeless and weary for us?

13. What does this reveal about the kind of leader Jeremiah was?

Verses 14-18

Notice Jeremiah's honest complaints and feelings as he reveals them to the Lord. Even in anguish he "sandwiches" his bitter feelings between praise and honor.

14. How do you usually handle trials in your life? With faith or fragility? Explain?

Meditate on Psalm 142.

15. What example does Jeremiah and King David set for us when we face trials and uncertainty?

16. What does this reveal about the character of God?

17. How can you experience God in a deeper way if you chose to praise Him during trials rather than just petition for rescue?

18. When you find yourself in a circumstance that is discouraging, doubtful, distasteful, one of waiting or longing, do you do your part to make it better or bitter?

God can handle our complaints and our heart's whining and sorrows. However, we must not get stuck in them and acknowledge that He has the power and the will to rescue us from our troubles in His good time. He is a personal God, A Father who is more concerned with our obedience and holiness than he is in our mere happiness; yet he is always ready to hand out mercy.

Fighter Verse:
"...His word is in my heart like a fire, a fire shut up in my bones. I am weary of holding it in; indeed, I cannot." Jeremiah 20:9

Prayer: Lord I pray that you set a fire down in my bones that I can't contain it; that everyone I meet would see the flame glowing bright in my life, passing from one heart to another.

Chapter 21

"The only thing necessary for the triumph of evil is for good men to do nothing."
~Edmund Burke

King Josiah	Babylon takes 1ˢᵗ wave of	Jehoiachin	King Zedekiah
641-609BC	608 BC	598-597BC	587 BC

Did you know:

King Zedekiah reigned only three months before the Babylonians captured and conquered Jerusalem. He was about twenty-one years old when he took office and refused to heed the instruction of Jeremiah.

As you can see from the timeline the book of Jeremiah is not chronological. Jeremiah tells the story going back in time referring to different times out of order. (You will soon find out why.)

Verses 1-2

1. What were the King's hopes?

Verses 3-7

2. What response do you think King Zedekiah had for Jeremiah's {not-so} politically correct words?

Verse 8

3. What does this reveal about God's will towards Jeremiah and all the leaders he calls?

**Truth is never relative, never subjective.
Truth is sharp- cutting through marrow.
It waits to be reckoned with;
it beams in darkness and yet so easy to ignore.
Once it is seen it calls us out and thrusts us into reflection,**

"What will I do with this?"
It causes the eyes to see, the ears to hear, the soul to know depth.
Truth doesn't rest and is never wrong.
Truth beckons a response.
Truth beckons change.

4. Even though at present we still enjoy *some* freedom to speak about our faith to others how prepared are you to live out your faith openly even if you are punished for it?

On a scale, how politically correct of a person are you?

| ⎯⎯ |

I am a politician   Only when I feel like it   I speak truth in all situations

5. Has the Lord ever put you in a situation where he needed you to say something or do something that was not very politically correct? What was the response around you?

Read:
____ Prov. 22:17-21
_____ Ephesians 4:11-15

6. What conditions must we follow in speaking truth?

7. What must be our motivation?

8. Think back to Jeremiah 20:1 when Pashhur beat and imprisoned Jeremiah. Do you suppose it was because he thought Jeremiah was ludicrous and prophesying falsely or cramping his complacent, spiritually-lazy style?

Read:
____ Deut. 18:20

9. What was the consequence of prophesying falsely?

10. Do you think God was concerned for Jeremiah's safety?

Read:
_____ Jeremiah 1:19

11. What promises did Jeremiah have to cling to in times of fear for his life?

Study the chart below.

Truth Speaker	Verses	Immediate Consequence of speaking Truth	Long-term effects of speaking truth
Paul 1.In Prison Rome 2.Last letter before death	Phil. 1:12-14 2 Tim. 4:6-8 2 Tim.4:17-18	Imprisonment Death	Gospel spreads all over Europe and Aisa
Jesus (Right before Crucifixion)	Jn. 18:33-38 Jn.11	Death	Christianity enters the world, salvation from death

Read:
____Matthew 28:19-20

12. These were Jesus' last words. What truth did He command the disciples to speak?

God's vow of protection may not look the way we think it should look. It is not always free of worry or struggle. Notice that he doesn't tell Jeremiah that they *won't* hurt him or that they *won't* attack him; God only promises that He will not allow the enemy to *overcome* him and that He will *rescue* and *save* him.

13. Have you ever doubted God's protection over you because it didn't line up with your idea of what protection should look like?

Protection may not come in the form of a white-picked fence in a gated community free from pollutants of the world or danger, hatred, hurt, loss, sickness or even a consistent paycheck. But we can rest assure that the Giver of life and death is the only one that can say when our time here on earth is up.

Verses 9-10

14. What conditions does the Lord put on the people?

15. How much faith do you think was required of the people to surrender to the Babylonians?

16. Was surrendering to a country that just set their country on fire a logical choice? Or did it seem more logical to flee to another country that would accept refugees and share their abundance with them?

Verses 11-14

17. What is God requiring of the Kingdom of Jerusalem in the midst of their punishment?

Fighter Verse:
Write out your favorite verse here.

Prayer:
Write out your prayer.

Chapter 22

Verses 1-2

1. What is the location where Jeremiah is supposed to deliver his message?

2. Who is his audience?

3. So far, the Lord has asked Jeremiah to speak to two different groups, who are they? (Read: Jeremiah 20:1 and Jeremiah 22:1)

Verse 3

4. Who is God asking them to protect?

Verse 4

5. What is the promise if they obey?

Verse 5

6. What are the consequences if they don't?

This isn't the first time God mentions protection for the alien, fatherless and widow in scripture:

"Religion that God our Father accepts as pure and faultless is this: look after orphans and widows in their distress..." James 1:27

"...defend the cause of the fatherless, plead the case of the widow." Isaiah 1:17

7. What does this reveal about God's heart for these groups of helpless people?

8. What action steps can you take to apply this kind of love in your heart for these groups of helpless people?

Alien:_____

Fatherless:_____

Widow:_____

Verses 6-9

This is both a poetic and prophetic statement. God compares the palace of the King of Judah as:

Gilead: "Mountainous", *pleasant (Matthew Henry)*
Lebanon: "Whiteness," lush, rich, grand

> God will still destroy her no matter how beautiful or grand she is. Make
> no mistake our beauty and charm will never save us from our sin. God will
> never overlook our offenses based on any of our superficial qualities.
> *Repentance is a must!*

Verse 10

9. What is being said about the king in this verse?

Did you know:

An ancient burial custom for Israel was to be buried with community and family. The Hebrew children of ancient days placed high value on being buried with their fathers in their own city. And it was a punishment not to be buried at all (Deut. 28:26). For a king not to be buried by his kin and much less in another city not his own was a great insult.

Verses 11-17

10. Who is Shallum (whose son)?

11. Why is the Lord rebuking King Jehaohaz, also known as Shallum? What hint do we get at what led him astray?

Read:
____2 Kings 23:1-3
____Jeremiah 22:15b-16

12. What kind of man was King Josiah (Shallum's father)?

Verses 18-23

13. Who is Jehoiakim?

14. What inference does this scripture make about the way he led God's people?

Verse 24

    15. Who is Jehoiachin?

Verses 24-30

    16. What are a few objects the Lord uses to refer to Jehoiachin as?

    17. What are the contrasts between King Josiah and his son's and grandson?

    18. Describe your spiritual upbringing.

    19. Have you personally made your faith your own or is your faith based on tradition? Explain.

    20. Have you had the opportunity to share your testimony with someone who doesn't know Jesus? Explain.

Take some time to reflect on when you were impacted by the Lord for the first time:

Write your testimony here:

Fighter Verse:

"Woe to him who builds his palace by unrighteousness, his upper rooms by injustice..." Jer. 22:13

Prayer:

Lord, may I stand up against injustice, may I defend the cause of the poor, alien, orphan and widow. Help me speak when I don't have the words. Convict my heart when I've walked too far away and may I speak truth whenever you put the opportunity in front of me. Amen

Chapter 23

Verses 1-2

1. Based on these verses what are the contrasts between good and bad shepherds?

Fill in the chart with your answers.

Bad Shepherds	Good Shepherds
	Protect their flock
	Draw them into the fold
	Give sound doctrine
	Restore the sheep

2. At this point you should be feeling the call toward leading others to Christ or closer to Christ. What does "shepherding" look like in your life? (Think of peers, younger women, children, co-workers, mentees, classmates, new-believers, etc.)

Read:
____Psalm 23:1-3
____Isaiah 40:11

3. Based on these verses what kind of Shepherd is God? Use descriptive words.

4. How has this been evident in your life? In what ways has He been a Shepherd to you?

Verses 3-4

5. What promise does God make towards His people?

Verses 5-6

6. Who is the "Righteous Branch" in this passage?
(Hint: refer to the margin of your Bible reference.)

Although God made and kept promises to **scatter** His people among the heathen nations (Leviticus 26:14-33) he also made a promise to **gather** them from all the nations where he scattered them. When God punishes he never intends to leave things as they are. Reconciliation is always the goal.

Read:
_____Deut. 30:1-3
_____Matt.23:37

Did you know:
Israel ceased to be a complete nation twice. Once in 587 BC after the Babylonian captivity and after the Roman Empire conquered it in 70 AD. If we could see it on a time line it would look like this:

God *gathers* people and makes Israel a nation	1st *scattering* (Northern Tribes) Assyrians	2nd *scattering* (Southern Tribes) Babylonians	God *gathers* Jews back to Promise Land	Israel *scattered* Romans	Israel est. (still being *gathered*)
1300s	722BC	587BC	517BC	70AD	1948
Joshua	2 Kings 17:5-6	Jeremiah	Ezra	The Epistles	

7. What does this reveal about God's active role in humanity?

8. What hope does this give us for the prophecies in the Bible that are still to come to pass?

Verses 7-8
Although Jeremiah did not get to see this magnificent prophecy come true he believed it would happen. He proclaimed it with unwavering faith!

Verses 9-14

9. What does this reveal about the cultural climate of Jeremiah's days?

10. Do you see any resemblance in modern times? Explain.

Verse 15

11. In light of Jesus being our Good Shepherd can you see why he would protect them from false prophets? How does this help your view of Him as Shepherd?

Verses 16-22

12. What are the symptoms of false prophets and false teachers?

A false prophet/teacher is someone who not only lies about the truth but someone who waters it down and gives "half-truths" for the sake of comfort. Being politically correct is the name of the game for false teachers. Beware of them and their message.

"We cannot be whole women on half-truths. Sisters, study the scriptures" ~ @Beth Moore

Verse 23-24

13. What claim does God make about himself? Meditate upon it.

Read:
____ Psalm 56:8
____Psalm 139:1-4
____Malachi 3:16

14. What does this reveal about God's knowledge of our secret places?

15. What does it reveal about His intimacy with *you*?

16. How does this truth impact you?

Verses 25-33

17. How are we to handle false doctrine about the Lord?

18. How do you discern false information?

Read:
____Matt. 23:1-4
____Matt. 23:23-26

19. How did Jesus handle false doctrine and those who delivered it?

Fighter Verse:

Prayer:
Lord, help me discern truth and speak truth when I need to. In the midst of cultural norms help me stand up against half-truths and lies. May I be a light in darkness and uphold your precepts in my heart. May I not waver in my convictions and keep them in the most difficult situations. May I speak in love that I may draw those that listen to You. Help me stay focused on you even when I feel alone and abandoned and the journey seems weary. Give me purpose in difficult relationships that I may love like you love and forgive like you forgive, in Jesus' precious name.

Chapter 24

Verse 1

1. What has taken place?

2. Who is included in the exile?

3. Where did the Lord speak to Jeremiah (location)?

Verse 2

4. What object was used to describe the people?

Did you know:
Figs were an important part of Israel's economic health and wealth. Figs are often referred to in the bible as a sign of prosperity as in Isaiah 36:16. When God takes the fig tree away it is usually a time of chastisement as in Hosea 2:12.

Verses 3-7

5. What was the vision Jeremiah had?

Reread:
____Jeremiah 1:10

6. What contrast of words do you see in Jer. 1:10 and Jer. 24:6

Read:
____Phil 1:4-6 (Emphasis on verse 6)

7. What promise do we have in this verse? Proclaim these in your prayer time today.

> If God calls us to someone it's because he's already started a work in them; he is merely using us to help complete it, whatever the outcome may be.

Read:

____Romans 5:6-8

8. What condition was humanity in when Christ died for us?

9. How does this affect your view of His love for you?

10. How does it affect the way you see others?

11. Who was a good fig while in captivity?

The story of a good fig:

Read:

____Ezra 1:1-4

____Ezra 7:6-10

12. What qualities set Ezra apart from other exiles?

13. Rewrite verse 10:

14. How was Ezra used in captivity to bring God's promises to fruition?

God's **Work cannot be a part from God's Word**. If we are called
to God's work His Word will always be needed!

Verses 8-10

15. Jeremiah gives the story away by telling us what happens to Jerusalem's last king. How does God describe him?

Refer back to Jer. 21:9. God told all the people to surrender to the Babylonians and not to stay in the city or they would die in Jerusalem by the hand of Nebuchadnezzar. This was another opportunity to obey and trust in their God, but old habits die-hard.

Read:

____2 Kings 17-18

16. What made Zedekiah a bad leader?

Read:

____2 Kings 24:20

17. Did Zedekiah obey the commands of the Lord? Explain.

If figs were considered to be an important part of life in Israel in ancient times what are your observations on why God would use the illustration of a 'bad fig' for the bad exiles?

There are several things we need in order to fulfill our calling:
God's favor, God's authority, and His Word. The good thing is
that if He's called us then He's already equipped us.

Fighter Verse:
I will set my eyes on them for good, and I will bring them back to this land. I will build them up, and not tear them down; I will plant them, and not pluck them up. I will give them a heart to know that I am the Lord, and they shall be my people and I will be their God, for they shall return to me with their whole heart. Jeremiah 24:6-7

Prayer:
Lord, grant me favor in the places you put me; let me recognize my authority in Christ with confidence. Teach me your Word that I may grow in knowledge and grace.

Chapter 25

Verses 1-3

1. How many years has Jeremiah been trying to lead the people to repentance?

2. How long did God have to wait for you until you surrendered your life to Him?

   This should remind us not give up on people simply because we cannot see the fruit in their life we want to see. We are not called to outcomes we are called to obedience.

   The Lord is not slow in keeping his promise, as some understand slowness. Instead he is patient with you, not wanting anyone to perish, but everyone to come to repentance.
   2 Peter 3:9

Verses 4-7

3. What were the prophets referred to as?

4. Why were the prophets given to the people for?

Verses 8-11

5. How does he refer to Nebuchadnezzar?

6. How many years does God promise to keep them in captivity?

Read:
_____Isaiah 8:5-7
_____Haggai 2:22

Did you know:
Assyria conquered all of Israel and part of Judah (refer back to timeline in chapter 21) for the same reasons we see in Jeremiah: hardened hearts, idolatry, and a lack of love for the One True God.

7. What does this reveal about God's sovereignty over all nations (even our enemies)?

Verses 12-14

8. What was the promise after the seventy years?

Verses 15-16

9. What was the message Jeremiah was to give the people?

Verses 17-29

10. Who was included in drinking from the cup of wrath?

11. What kind of expectations did God place on Jeremiah to tell the people this news?

Jeremiah didn't go to every nation and actually offer them a sip of wine. This prophecy was either, written and sent in a letter or prophesized publicly.

Verses 30-38

12. What hard truth was lying in the hands of Jeremiah?

13. What do you think will happen to Jeremiah if he speaks the truth?

14. How does speaking the truth about the gospel conflict with modern-day culture?

15. What are you willing to face for speaking truth for Christ? How far are you willing to go for the One True God? Are you willing to lose your career, material comforts, friends, popularity, your life for the one who gave it all up for you?

16. What kind of faith did Jeremiah have in order to deliver a message that had not yet played out?

Read:
____Acts 28:17-30

Paul is speaking to the Roman government about faith in Jesus at a time when Christians were being martyred for their faith. The crime of sharing your faith was punishable by death in the most torturous ways. The Roman government got to determine the type of death you would receive. Some Christian's were boiled to death, some eaten by lions while they were still alive, others stoned, or lit on fire to decorate Herod's palace. Fear didn't stop Paul, the fear of not doing it was greater than death itself.

17. What characteristics did Paul possess in order to speak truth to the Roman government and to his people?

On a scale how bold are you in proclaiming truth to others?

l–l———10-l
Chicken flies the coupe   Telling it on a mountain!

18. How can you *'plant'* Paul's type of boldness in your walk to lead others to Christ?

19. Is there someone in your circle of influence that He is asking you to speak truth to?

20. What steps can you take to accomplish this mission?

"We are settling for a Christianity that revolves around catering to ourselves when the central message of Christianity is actually about abandoning ourselves."
~David Platt-
Radical-Taking Back Your Faith from the American Dream

Fighter Verse:
The clamor will resound to the ends of the earth,
for the Lord has an indictment against the nations;
he is entering into judgment with all flesh,
and the wicked he will put to the sword, declares the Lord.

Prayer:
Lord, allow me to use my God-given talents, gifts and personality to share the gospel and hope of Jesus Christ with those you put in my life. May I be sensitive to the prompting of the Holy Spirit and open to new opportunities in leading others to you. May my life be a lamp for the lost and hope for the weary.

Chapter 26

"True intercession involves bringing the person, or the circumstance that seems to be crashing in on you, before God, until you are changed by His attitude toward that person or circumstance. People describe intercession by saying, "It is putting yourself in someone else's place." That is not true! Intercession is putting yourself in God's place; it is having His mind and His perspective."
— Oswald Chambers

in·ter·cede:
verb
to intervene on behalf of another; mediate; to interpose on behalf of someone during a time of difficulty by pleading or petitioning.

Verse 1

1. Refer back to the timeline in week five. What year does this chapter take place?

Verses 2-6
Same place, same faces, same message.

1. Do you ever feel like it is impossible to reach the lost around you? That despite your best efforts you still can't get through? Explain.

Sometimes the only explanation of the gospel that we have is the way we live.

Verse 5
You're not alone!

Jeremiah isn't the only godly man sent to *intercede* for God's people.

Plot these great men and women of the faith on the timeline according to the time the Lord used them in history. (**Dates are close approximations)

Moses 1444BC
Rahab 1406 BC

Isaiah 700BC
Jeremiah 601 BC
Daniel 530 BC
Esther 400 BC
Paul 60AD

(Your name)

|———————————————————————————————————————|

Look at all these people! They were all ordinary people called to do extraordinary things for God; all imperfect, living out their calling right where God placed them. Your name is on the timeline. Your journey is yet to be finished.

2. Do you see yourself placed here on earth, at this time in history to intercede on behalf of God's people and for the lost around you?

3. What goals do you have in reaching people for Christ? Explain.

Read:
____Galatians 1:15-16a

4. What did Paul feel set apart for?

Meditate on Paul's calling and pray to the Lord that it also becomes your calling.

Verse 7-11

5. What did they threaten to do to Jeremiah?

Read:
____Matt 26:57-68

6. How does Jeremiah's life and the life of Jesus parallel?

Verse 12-15

7. Did Jeremiah relent on his mission?

8. What does this say about his faith in God and relationship with the Almighty?

9. What intentional step can you take this week to apply this kind of faith to a situation in your life? Write it out and share it.

Verse 16-19

10. What observations can you make on how God uses others to stop the hand of the enemy in order to protect His mission so that it can prevail? Do other stories in the bible come to mind? Which ones?

Verse 20

11. Who is the man who also prophesied at the same time as Jeremiah?

Verse 21-23

Sometimes following God and sacrificing our lives for Him does not get the end result we desire. God uses all willing members of the body to help advance the gospel. Even though Uriah does not have a book in his name and did not live to see the return of his people 70 years later; by obedience His life did glorify God. We can rest assure that he fulfilled his purpose on earth and he did not die in vain. As we've learned through this study not one life is taken without God's permission. At the end of Uriah's life we know it was his time to go Home. This gives us faith to know that our days are numbered by our Creator- that our end and anything in between is not a surprise to Him

Verse 24

12. Why do you think Jeremiah was not put to death alongside Uriah?

13. How did God rescue Jeremiah from death?

Fighter Verse:

Then Jeremiah spoke to all the officials and all the people, saying, "The Lord sent me to prophesy against this house and this city all the words you have heard. Now therefore mend your ways and your deeds, and obey the voice of the Lord your God, and the Lord will relent of the disaster that he has pronounced against you. Jeremiah 26:12&13

Prayer:

Lord, help me see my place in history, help me grasp my calling, my purpose, my mission. Give me wisdom to prioritize my life and daily comings and goings that I may seek you at every corner. I pray for the ones you've placed in my life that I need to intercede for. Give me the words I need to speak and the love I must show. Amen.

Chapter 27

Verse 2
A yoke is a curved wooden beam placed on the backs of oxen to plough fields. In this verse it is used figuratively to mean "oppression."

1. What does God ask Jeremiah to do?

2. What demonstration was he trying to make?

Read:
____Matt: 11:28-30

Burdens can be scars from the past, self-sufficiency, depression, anger, anxiety, fear, control, mistrust, pride of life, work, mismanaged time etc.

1. Are *you* carrying a heavy burden that is too heavy for you? What is it?

2. After carrying such a burden what should we do with it?

3. What led to God's people being "yoked"?

Check the correct response.

____God's harshness towards his people
____The people's refusal to heed to God's gentle hand

Read Romans 11:32.
God never pushes us to sin but he will allow it in order to get our attention.
His hope is that when we become emptied and unsatisfied we'll look
up- to the one who can truly fill and satisfy. His mercy awaits!

Verses 3-4
(Location of Edom, Moab, Ammom)

Fig. 1

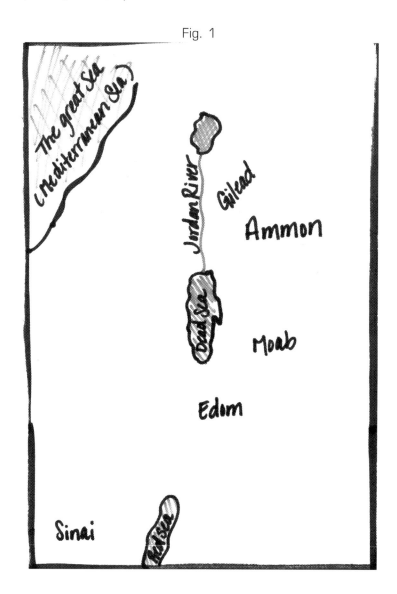

For reference:
Mark your map in Figure 1, with a T (Tyre), body of water above Jabesh-Gilead. Then mark S (Sidon) north of your T. Sidon was about 25 miles from Tyre.

Verse 5

4. What claims does God make about himself here?

5. What connection does this statement have with verses 3 and 4?

Verses 6-11

6. What prophetic statements does Jeremiah make about Babylon?

Ancient Babylon had a turbulent past, rising up to its full glory and then falling to Assyrian power then to rise again by the hand of the Chaldean, Nebuchadnezzar. It is no coincidence that it was Nebuchadnezzar, at this time in history 604-561BC, who returned Babylon to her prior glory in order that God's plan for His people might prevail. This truth brings relevancy to the Bible proving that God's words have been proven true by archeologists and historians alike time and time again.

Verse 11

7. What lesson might God have for those who bow down to the heavy yoke of Nebuchadnezzar?

8. Is God asking you to intercede on behalf of someone bowing to a heavy burden? Pray for them through prayer during your prayer time.

God's ultimate plan for them {us} was and continues to be to experience how light his yoke is in relation to bondage. If you are struggling right now during times of oppression surrender it to the only One who can break it off. We weren't designed to control the things that are too heavy for us. If there is a lesson to be learned ask 'what?' If there is habit to break, then break it, an area of your life that needs to change, change it, if there is something zapping you of your energy for God, STOP IT! And put on the yoke of God and be free!

Verses 12-16

There are plenty of groups in our society (the church included) who are convinced our God does not punish and that He is merely a God of prosperity. Some believe He is not worthy of worship because He is merely a God that punishes. Some ask how can a God of love allow such atrocities in humanity? And yet the same question should be asked How can a Holy God allow such atrocities in humanity and turn His holy eye. There must be punishment for those who hurt children, who murder, steal, cheat, destroy. He is a God who bares pain so that offenders may know Him one day. He is the One always thinking about grace both for the offender and the offended. By His definition, grace overlooks what we deserve and gives us what we so desperately need. Grace by its very essence, is for offenders, sinners, you, and me; It's no wonder God is so patient to administer justice before giving time for mercy! That's grace.

Verse 17-22

9. What are the "things" left in the house of the Lord (refer back to Jer. 27:19)?

10. What do these objects represent in the lives of God's people?

11. Can you recall a time when God's presence felt distant in your life? Explain.

Although God removed his physical presence from the people He gave them someone who would reveal God's love and commitment to them, someone to communicate God's will and commands to them, and someone to speak truth for God on His behalf. He shows us too, that we don't need physical reminders of his presence, like idols, or trinkets, we have His Living Word- the best reminder of all!

[1]*"...Having the reality of God's presence is not dependent on our being in a particular circumstance or place, but is only dependent on our determination to keep the Lord before us continually. Our problems arise when we refuse to place our trust in the reality of His presence. The experience the psalmist speaks of— "We will not fear, even though . . ." (Psalm 46:2)— will be ours once we are grounded on the truth of the reality of God's presence, not just a simple awareness of it, but an understanding of the reality of it. Then we will exclaim, "He has been here all the time!" At critical moments in our lives it is necessary to ask God for guidance, but it should be unnecessary to be constantly saying, "Oh, Lord, direct me in this, and in that." Of course He will, and in fact, He is doing it already! If our everyday decisions are not according to His will, He will press through them, bringing restraint to our spirit. Then we must be quiet and wait for the direction of His presence."*

Fighter Verse:
"Do not listen to the words of the prophets who are saying to you, 'You shall not serve the king of Babylon,' for it is a lie that they are prophesying to you. I have not sent them, declares the Lord, but they are prophesying falsely in my name, with the result that I will drive you out and you will perish, you and the prophets who are prophesying to you." Jeremiah 27:14-15

Prayer:
Lord help me not accept falsities about your word. Help me accept your nature and character, faithful and just. Help me accept when culture is wrong even when it is hard to see or admit.

---

[1] My Utmost for His Highest, July 20th 2014

Chapter 28

Verse 1

1. Who was the prophet spoken of in this verse and who was present?

Verse 2-4

2. What was the message?

Read:
___Jeremiah 25:11

3. How did the message contradict Jeremiah's?

Verses 5-9

4. How did Jeremiah respond?

5. What insight do we get about Jeremiah's attitude towards Hananiah?
(Remember the law about prophesying falsely.)

Verses 8-9

6. Why do you suppose God mostly sends prophets to speak truth during times of war, disaster, and plague?

Throughout scripture God warns His people that harm is coming their way- giving them ample time to *acknowledge* their sin, *repent*, and *return*. God uses ordinary men, often fretted with insecurities, called prophets, to intercede on behalf of the God Almighty and His people. Many great men of God have gone before us and sacrificed their lives so that we can have truth in our hands and eternity in our souls.

Prophet: as men filled with the spirit of God who by God's authority and command
in words of weight pleads the cause of God and urges salvation of men.
- Blue Letter Bible

Read:

____Acts 3:22-25

   7. Who is the ultimate prophet and what does that make us?

   8. What does this make us?

Verses 10-11

   9. What did Hananiah do?

Read:

____Matthew 16:21-23

   10. What did Jesus tell Peter when His words went against the will of God?

   11. How should we respond to falsehoods and pacifying lies about God's word?

Do you know anyone like this? Ones who can't stand the inconvenient truth of judgment, consequence for immorality and sin so they water down the truth and preach only "grace" as a way to get under the trappings of sinful behavior or past sin that hasn't been dealt with?

> Remember sin is sin no matter what generation you grew up in, what culture you're immersed in, what country you live in, your political affiliation- no matter the color of your skin; we are all measured by the same measure of Holiness- God's Holiness.

   12. Is there a misconception you believed about God that is inconsistent with His word? Explain.

Verses 12-17
God always has the last word. We can either find ourselves in His grace or on the side of judgment. In order to find grace, we must be first willing to obey.

Hananiah was hoping to escape judgment by sixty-eight years and lying to the people by making them believe that peace was around the corner. Hananiah is part of a camp of cowards who can't face the reality of their own sin. They want to pretend as though their actions have no effect on God or others. Sometimes the truth hurts but it always sets us free. If he had accepted the consequences of his sin he would have lived to see prosperity.

Has there been a time in your life when God allowed you to struggle through some trials but you were also able to see His promise at the end of it? Or are you still struggling on the journey waiting to see His promise for you? Explain.

Read:

____Hebrews 12:7

13. Instead of escaping discipline how does God expect us to handle His discipline?

Read:
____Prov. 13:24
____Prov. 19:18
____Prov. 23:13

14. What does God expect of us toward disciplining our own children?

15. How did the Lord speak to you through this lesson?

16. Have you made progress in praying for someone in your life who desperately needs it? Has there been any movement towards sharing Christ with someone in your circle who desperately needs it?

"God's definition of what matters is pretty straightforward.
He measures our lives by how we love."
~Francis Chan, Crazy Love: Overwhelmed by a Relentless God

Pray for that person and opportunity right now.

Fighter Verse:
"And Jeremiah the prophet said to the prophet Hananiah, "Listen, Hananiah, the Lord has not sent you, and you have made this people trust in a lie. Therefore thus says the Lord: 'Behold, I will remove you from the face of the earth. This year you shall die, because you have uttered rebellion against the Lord.'" Jeremiah 28:15&16 ESV

Prayer:
Lord, help me not accept lies over truth simply for comfort or inconvenience. May I be a game-changer in my generation. Make me a truth speaker- an intercessor for those who need you.

Chapter 29

Verses 1-3

1. Where was Jeremiah when he wrote this letter?

2. Who were the recipients?

Verses 4-9

3. What message was God instructing?

4. How much faith did this require from the exiles, living in a foreign land in bondage, starved, beaten, and almost dead? What was God's plan for them?

Verses 10-14

Fill in the chart of all the promises God makes in these verses and next to it write down what it says about his character.

God Promises	God's Character
I will visit you...	
Bring you back...	

Remember:

These promises were made during captivity. They had already committed atrocities in the name of other gods, sacrificed their living children and God is still pursuing them. He is meeting them right where they are. This is proof that He loves people even when they are in sin. It doesn't mean He agrees with their sin; it means that His love is not conditional upon whether we agree or not or whether we sin or not. It proves that He loves us so much that He won't stay away from us even when we are at our worst.

Verses 11-12

5. How does God use Jeremiah to send hope to the exiles?

Read:
____Lamentations 5:8-12

6. After reading a snapshot in the lives of the captives how do you think they took the words of Jeremiah?

Think of the exiles; they must have wanted to give up all hope because death was better than life. It was a hard lesson to learn for abandoning God's precepts. Perhaps the lesson was to see how gracious God's commands in comparison to those of Nebuchadnezzar.

7. Is there someone in your life you can pray Jeremiah 29:11-12 for?

8. How does this verse show God's protection and hope over His children even during trials and hardships?

9. What does this reveal about God's heart towards his children even during disobedience?

"Lukewarm people don't really want to be saved from their sin; they want only to be saved from the penalty of their sin."
— Francis Chan, Crazy Love: Overwhelmed by a Relentless God

Read:
____Malachi 3:16

Malachi was written after the time of Jeremiah and after the captivity in Babylon and again we see the people's hearts grow wicked once again. And yet God does not give up on them, what is he doing in heaven?

10. What picture do you draw of your heavenly Father based on this verse?

Read:
____Romans 15:13

11. What word in this verse defines part of God's character?

12. Do you give up easy when your faith walk is difficult? Is it easier to settle for complacency or is easier to draw nearer to Christ?

Explain.

Read:
____Hebrews 11:1

13. What should you cling to in times of hopelessness?

Think of someone in your life you hope salvation for one day. Pray Hebrews 11:1 for them. Fill in the blanks with their name(s). NLT

Faith is the confidence that (_____) will one day know Jesus Christ; it gives {me} assurance that God also wants _____ to come to know Him and that He has a plan for _____ although I cannot see it.

Verses 15-19
After all this time they still chose to live apart from God!

Jesus is a relentless God, pursuing even to depths. He will not let us go until we refuse on our last breath. He loves us unto the death. He will not quit until He rescues us. We can wrestle with Him but it doesn't make sense- He has the power to overwhelm. We might as well give in.

Verses 20-23

14. How does he use Zedekiah as an example of what happens to trusted "godly" leaders who lead God's people astray?

Verses 24-32
No lie about God gets past Him especially when people are being led astray.
Jeremiah takes it personal as should we.

15. How do you take lies about God when you hear them? Are you use to it? Or do you take it personal?

16. Do you think you have a responsibility to step-in when you hear someone speak a lie about God's word? (Explain)

Read:
____James 3:1
____2 Peter 2:1-2

17. According to James and Peter what are the cautions for teachers and those who lead God's people?

18. What does this reveal about the importance placed on leadership positions?

Fighter Verse:
(write out Jeremiah 29:11-12)

Prayer:

1. (Pray Jeremiah 29:13-14 for someone in your life that doesn't know Jesus)

2. Jesus, may I hold my calling in high regard just as you do. May I take it personal when I hear lies about your character and Word. Show me how and when to step-in and give me the words to speak to lead people towards you instead of away from you. Give me opportunities to show Christ's love to others. In your Son's name!

Chapter 30

Verses 1-2

   1. What did God have Jeremiah do?

Verse 3

   2. Why did He have him do that?

Read:
____2 Timothy 3:16a

   3. What confidence do we have in the written word of God?

Read:
____Matt 24:3-4
____Acts 7:11

   4. What is the importance of the written word of God?

> Speaking God's Word is essential for the Christian faith; we cannot help others see Christ if we do not speak about Him. Praying God's Word is the weapon we use to fight for those who do not yet know Him.
> We'll never know the reality of God's presence in our life if we don't devote a part of it to prayer. We will never experience the joy of participating in the great work of Heaven if we never help bring a soul to Christ.

Read:
____Matt. 24:30-31

   5. What correlation do you see from Jer. 30:3 and this verse?

Verse 4-7
There is no peace in punishment but there is hope; God's discipline does not last forever.

Verse 8

6. What is their promise?

Verses 9-10

7. Who is the king God is speaking of? (Read the following verses to confirm your answer.)

Read:
____Isaiah 11:1
____Luke 3:31b&32

Verse 11

8. What does this say about His faithfulness to His beloved Israel?

v.12-15

9. According to this verse who can save God's people?

Sin is incurable, deathly, only The Great Physician can provide remedy. All of life's problems are wrapped up in this verse. And the answer is only found in One, Jesus Christ. We must carry his message to others so that they may have a chance for healing.

10. How does this reality impact your urgency to bring the good news to those around you?

Name several people in your life who need the healing of the Savior.
1.
2.
3.

Verses 16-24
11. How does this relate to you? How can you apply these words in your life?

God doesn't want us to stay stuck in the condemning whispers of our past. There is hope for that old girl. With Christ we can be made new. When your past creeps up on you, you can always remind it of this reality: it is in the depths of the oceans, forgotten forever and be assured that it isn't your Heavenly Father whispering those things in your ears.

Read:
____Psalm 103:12
____Micah 7:18-19

12. What assurance can you offer those you intercede for that their sins are not too big for God to forgive?

The world says: "The past can never be erased." The stain will always be there, the damage has already been done."

13. Read Joel 2:25. What does God's word say about the years we lose for sin?

Forgiveness is not an option in God's economy. He died for it. The way God forgives you is the same way He forgives others. When God forgives He does so with a reward in mind- a new life and repayment of lost years.

As we reflect on God's relentless pursuit of obstinate people we should be reminded of how much He loves those in our lives (including ourselves) that are not that easy to love…or forgive.

14. Is there someone you need forgive that you haven't completely forgiven?

Intercession is not only about God forgiving others; it sometimes includes us having to forgive them too. Keep in mind those you may not have forgiven in the past and present.

Challenge:
1.) pray for those you listed above
2.) forgive someone who has hurt you
Forgiveness Exercise: Write a letter forgiving someone who has hurt you. Enclose it in an envelope. Pray over the envelop and continue to pray over it until you have been released of the unforgiveness. In some situations, it may be effective to share with the offender in others it might be more helpful to keep it between you and the Lord during your prayer time.

For if you forgive other people when they sin against you, your heavenly Father will also forgive you. ~Matthew 6:14

Blessed are the merciful, for they will be shown mercy. ~Matthew 5:7

Be kind and tender-hearted to one another, forgiving each other just as in Christ God forgave you. ~Ephesians 4:32

Fighter Verse:
"And it shall come to pass in that day, declares the Lord of hosts, that I will break his yoke from off your neck, and I will burst your bonds, and foreigners shall no more make a servant of him.[a] But they shall serve the Lord their God and David their king, whom I will raise up for them."
Jeremiah 30:8&9

Prayer:

Lord, thank you for promising Jesus so long ago and fulfilling it. You are a God of promise, a God of forgiveness and reconciliation, no matter the depths. Forgive me when I take that for granted. Help me live today with reconciliation in my heart.

Chapter 31

in·flu·ence

noun

noun: **influence**; plural noun: **influences**

the capacity to have an effect on the character, development, or
behavior of someone or something, or the effect itself.

Verses 1-2

1. By reading the context of this verse what does *"at that time"* mean? At what time?

Verse 3-9

What a celebration it will be on the day the Lord gathers and rebuilds Israel!

Read:
____Lamentations 3:22-23
____Luke 15:6-7
____Luke 15:13-24

2. What does this reveal about the heart of God towards his children who return? What does it say about his hope for them?

3. Is it strange to think that God himself *hopes* for His children, His people, for us? Since He is God can't He just control us and make us submit instead of *hope* we would? What does this reveal about His nature?

4. Have you given up hope for someone in your life? How can you be more like Christ in this area?

Verse 10

5. Who is God's audience and what does He want them to know?

Look at the chart to compare our God to other major religions.

Religion	Description	Flaws
Islam	One God, distant, judgment based on works and religious devotion. In order to find mercy one must perform 5 duties to prove their faithfulness.	Man depends on own strength to meet spiritual duties. God is impersonal and unknowable. The credibility of Islam is based on one man's word and vision, thus having only 1 prophet to allege the word of Allah.
Hinduism	Many gods. Judgment is based on deeds and works.	No moral code or law of conduct. All is relative. What is good for one may not be for another. Leaves the questions: What is good? And why isn't one god good enough?
Buddhism	No god. Strives for spiritual perfection through self-control of sensual desires through self-discipline through meditation.	Depends on one's own strength and leaves the question who am I meditating to if there is no God?
New Age	I am God. God is in everything. All paths lead to eternity.	I am God. If all religions are right then most of them are wrong because every religion believes they are the way to eternity or there is no such thing.
Christianity	One God. Personal, loving, forgiving, humble yet mighty. He is powerful enough to answer all our questions and prayers and workout divine circumstances in one's life and needs no other gods for help. Answers all questions for sin. Gives man a purpose and way to eternal life without earning it as humanity has proven it can't anyway.	It's a personal choice. It requires acknowledgement of sinful nature and acceptance of God's salvation. The cost of following Christ is high. We must weigh it before we accept it.

6. Compared to other religions what characteristics of our God impresses your heart the most?

Read:

____Isaiah 40:11

____Ezekiel 34:23

____John 10:11

7. After reading these scriptures and studying the chart above what sets our God apart from all the others?

8. Does this help you defend your faith more readily when tempted to question whether another religion might have the answers to life's major questions?

9. How prepared do you feel to answer the question: what is the difference between Christianity and other religions?

But in your hearts revere Christ as Lord. Always be prepared to give an answer to everyone who asks you to give the reason for the hope that you have. But do this with gentleness and respect. . .".
1 Peter 3:15

Verses 10-14

10. Israel is referred to as a well-watered garden (v.12) and that they will be filled with God's bounty (v.14b). Is the Lord merely talking about material provisions?

Read:
___John 4:13-14
___Rev. 22:1-3

Now, refer back to Jeremiah 2:13. God accused His people of two sins:

1. Forsaking him,' the spring of living water' (v.13a)

2. Digging their own cisterns (v.13b)

3. Now read Jeremiah 22:17. Who is referred to as the living water?

> God's hope for His children and all of humanity is that one
> day we would all accept His Living Water.

4. How has God's Living Water made a difference in your life? Is it worth sharing?

Verse 15
Always weeping for Israel!

Rachel, a matriarch of the Jewish faith is used as a prophetic metaphor to describe the pain and anguish during the times of King Herod when Christ is born and orders the death of all new born boys. Matthew 2:17&18

Can you imagine the legacies lost through the death of so many Hebrew babies? This wasn't the first time Hebrew children faced threats of death by enemy forces. Throughout history we see the hand of the enemy heavy upon God's people. Satan and his minions will stop at nothing to make sure Godly legacies die. Whether it be by watering down the truth, convincing us that biblical matters are not as serious as God makes them out to be or by distracting us with all the burdens and luxuries of our times. Whatever the case maybe we must stand against the tidal wave of complacency and affirm that God's word is important today as it was when it was written.

Verses 16-17

5. What does God promise after discipline?

    1. R_____ them for their work. (v.16b)
    2. R_____ them from the land of their enemy. (v. 16b)
    3. Provide H_____ for their future. (v. 17)

Verses 18-20 (NIV)
Reflect and meditate on the chart below and put yourself in Ephraim's place.

When I. . .	God. . .
(Ephraim)	
Rebel	Disciplines
Return	Restores
Stray	Speaks against me And hopes for my return
Repent	Yearns and has compassion for me

After reading the chart put your thoughts about God here:

Verses 21-22

6. What directions does the Lord give the wanderers?

7. Is your heart prone to wander? In what ways can you set up "road signs" and "guideposts" to keep you from wandering? How do you stay accountable for your walk with God? What practices do you have in place to keep your heart faithful?

8. How can you be a godly {guidepost} influence in someone else's life? Give examples? Do you currently play this role in someone else's life?

Verses 23-26

9. How was this message revealed to Jeremiah?

Verses 27-28

10. Refer back to Jeremiah 1:10. How do we see the full circle of these verses?

Verses 29 *It's my parent's fault!*
'The Fathers have eaten sour grapes and the children's teeth are set on edge.'

This was a common saying and belief in ancient times in the Jewish faith. It's meaning comes from the belief that children inherit the sins of their fathers. If a father sins the children will pay the consequences and continue to live in that way to no fault of their own. It was a way for people to blame their present sin on their parents.

Ponder for a moment:

11. Have you ever blamed your parents for the way you turned out? What mistakes can you own and take back from your parents? Loaded question? This one may take some time to digest especially when blaming our parents is so easy. We must take full responsibility for our own sin and not place it on the backs of our parents. Don't worry there is freedom in this too. Your children can't blame you for their sin! Relieved? So am I!

Write out a few of your bad behaviors that you blame on your parents. Pray over them. Acknowledge the part you play and the ability to stop. Own up, confess, and move on! It'll be a freeing experience once it's over. Remember God holds us all accountable for our heart issues. We won't get to blame mom or pops or a lack their-of when we see Him face to face.

Verses 31-34

12. What does this say about the type of covenant God expects from His worshippers?

13. How is this type of religion different than the type passed down from the patriarchs in verse 29?

14. Is God's Word in your heart and mind? Explain.

Verses 35-37

15. What claims is God making about himself? Affirm it with the chart on page 111.

Verse 38
God redeems! Amen!

God uses Nehemiah to rebuild the temple that was destroyed by the Babylonians. He always has a plan, a purpose and a promise.

Verse 39

Nowhere else in the bible are these locations given in scriptures. It must be a prophetic statement of things to come.

Gareb: "Scabby" (a hill near Jerusalem in the southwest)

Goah: "Bellowing"

Verse 40

Kidron Valley: "Dark" (also known as the place where the dead bodies of Hebrew children were dumped during sacrifice to Baal.)

If we take the definitions of locations of the new temple we can see how God repairs and redeems the broken, dark, scabby, and painful places we bring ourselves to. Only He can make a New Jerusalem out of the slums human nature creates. What we make for evil He redeems for glory!

Fighter Verse:

"...I will put my law in their minds and write it on their hearts. I will be their God and they will be my people." Jeremiah 31:33

Prayer:

Lord, redeem the dark, scabby, and painful places in my heart. Help me take responsibility for my own sin so that I may not hinder those I lead to you. Heal me from past wounds and set me free of their strong holds.

Chapter 32

Verse 1

1. Refer back to your timeline on page 70. Find the year of Zedekiah's reign. About what year did this chapter take place?

Verse 2

2. What was the political climate of this time?

Verses 3-5

3. Where is Jeremiah at this time and why is he there?

Verses 6-13

4. What did God instruct Jeremiah to do?

5. What kind of faith did Jeremiah must have in order to purchase land in a place that was about to be destroyed?

6. Has the Lord ever asked you to do something that seemed illogical? What was your response and action?

Verses 14-23

7. Notice Jeremiah 's prayer pattern, what is he acknowledging about God?

8. How do you usually start your prayers?

____Asking God for things
____Lifting up people in your life
____Thanking Him
____Acknowledging His greatness

9. How can you apply the same prayer pattern that Jeremiah used the next time you pray?

10. How would you respond today if God were to ask you to do something that didn't make sense and had no logical reason?

Verses 24-25 *Praise Him in the questioning!*

> David praised Him in turmoil, Daniel praised him in the lion's den, Paul praised him in prison, Jeremiah praised Him in questioning.

11. How do you praise God at your worst?

12. What do you think everyone thought of Jeremiah buying land in a city that was about to be destroyed?

13. What influence/example was he setting for God's people?

On a scale, what kind of influence do you tend to have on people?

| |———————————————————————————————————| |

Worldly	Passive	Godly
(Sinful)	(Complacent/Fearful)	(Faithful)

"You are the light of the world. A town built on a hill cannot be hidden. Neither do people light a lamp and put it under a bowl. Instead they put it on its stand, and it gives light to everyone in the house. In the same way, let your light shine before others, that they may see your good deeds and glorify your Father in heaven." Matthew 5:14-16 NIV

Verses 26-35

14. Notice the pattern of God's answer.

15. What does God *remind* Jeremiah of?

16. Do you ever feel that God gives repetitive answers/reminders to your prayers?

Verses 36-44

17. Notice what comes after God's reminding. What does he *reassure* Jeremiah of?

Share with your group if there is something in your life that God continues to reassure you of.

Fighter Verse:

"I am the Lord, the God of all mankind. Is anything too hard for me?"
Jer.32:27

Prayer:

Chapter 33

Verse 1

1. Where is Jeremiah?

Verses 2-3

2. Before He reveals the message of the Lord what does he reveal about God? How does he describe Him?

3. Focus on verse 3, what claim does God make about himself?

4. How can you take advantage of His amazing resource?

> The amazing thing about Christianity is that you don't have to have all the answers to people's questions. You just need to point them to the One who has all the answers and know in your heart He will answer them.

> Your Influence has more power than you realize.
> When you follow Christ- people are watching.

Verses 4-13

5. How can you represent this doctrine to someone who is doubting God's goodness or who is convinced that God is merely a judgmental God with no mercy?

6. Have you believed and received that God is a merciful God? Is there something that you are going through that is holding you back from accepting His mercy? What specific areas are you struggling with?

> "...Flocks again will pass under the hand of the One who counts them, says the Lord." Jer. 33:13

7. What view of God did you have of God growing up? Does it differ from what you've learned so far? Explain.

Verses 14-16

8. What/who is promised to Israel and to Judah?

Verses 17-22

Although, historically the Israelites proved to be unfaithful, idolatrous, and rebellious, God made a promise that David's throne would never sit empty. However, after the fall of Babylon no one ever actually sat on the throne again. Who is the 'one' he is referring to? Read Acts 2:25-35 for reference.

Verses 23-26

We serve a God who is not flaky, not passive, not complacent, not nonchalant about His people. When he makes a promise he keeps it- for all eternity. He is infinite, faithful, passionate, active, loving, and He calling you into a deeper knowledge and intimacy with Him. But this knowledge is not just for you to enjoy. He wants you to share it with those who don't understand it. Will you do it?

9. Everyone has influence. Name all the areas of your life you have influence.

(Think of marriage, children, friends, family, neighbors, social groups, community groups etc.)

1.
2.
3.
4.
5.
6.
7.
8.

"Everyone has influence. We all influence someone. And God expects us to be good stewards of that influence for His kingdom's sake. He didn't give us our influence for selfish purposes on our part, but so that we might share the good news about him – so that we could be Kingdom builders..."

"I am eternally accountable for how I used the influence God gave me in this life. What I do with my influence in the temporary world matters forever, and the Bible is filled with proof of this. The question God will ask every human being in His judgment is, "What did you do with my Son, Jesus?" And the question He will ask everyone who is a member of His family is, "What did you do with the time and the resources and the influence I gave you?"

I want to influence this world in light of the next. That's our calling as Kingdom builders!"
~Rick Warren

10. In light of your spiritual gifts name ways you can become more active in becoming a Kingdom builder?

11. What areas can you serve in that will put your spiritual gifts to work?

Fighter Verse:

Prayer:

Lord, help me receive my responsibility to influence those around me. Empower me to use my gifts, talents, and personality, to influence those around me to you.

Chapter 34

Verse 1

1. What is happening at this moment in history?

Veses 2-7

2. What promise and hope did he offer Zedekiah although he did not deserve it?

Verses 8-16
Even during turmoil God's people choose to disobey.

3. Is there an area of your life God continues to ask you to be faithful, obedient and it is tempting to renege on your promise to Him? Explain.

4. What steps can you take towards obedience in this area? Write them out.

Verses 17-22

5. What does God do in response to their disobedience?

In ancient time when two parties entered into an agreement they would seal their commitment to each other by cutting an animal in half to symbolically proclaim, "May I be like this animal cut in two if I break this covenant."

Read:
____Gen. 15:5-22
____Gal.3:29

6. How does the covenant with Abraham apply to you?

7. What does your covenant relationship with Jesus look like (also referred to as the Covenant of Grace)? What promises have you made when you gave your life over to Him?

Read:

____Eph. 4:20-24 (read 20-32 for further meditation)

____1 John 1:7

____1 John 2:3-5

8. The cost to follow Christ is high. When you accepted Christ, you made a commitment to leave the old you behind. Is your promise still relevant? How can you make it relevant on a daily basis?

> The cool thing is that we aren't made new or different on our own strength
> or merit nor do either of those worthless things carry us on after our
> relationship with God grows. Our strength will tire, our beauty will fade,
> our good works will be challenged with challenging people;
> thankfully it is the Spirit that lives in us that gives us the capacity to change, to
> desire good things, to say no to bad things and keep moving forward in Christ.

Fighter Verse:

Those who have violated my covenant and have not fulfilled the terms of the covenant they made before me, I will treat like the calf they cut in two and then walked between its pieces. Jeremiah 34:18

Prayer:

Lord, give me a sincere heart for your Word- what is written. Help me not take our relationship for granted.

Chapter 35

Verse 1

Notice that this verse goes back in time to King Jehoiakim's reign, more than ten years before the fall of Babylon.

Verses 2-16

1. How and why does the Lord choose to use this family as an example to the rebellious, complacent people?

Imagine the culture the Recabites were living in- total disobedience, the distortion of the Jewish faith, the blending with heathens and murderers. And yet they managed to stand firm in God, which made an impression on the heart of God.

2. H t was for them to keep their faith when all of their Jewish peers were following the ways of the world? Do you see any similarities in current times?

On a scale how radical is your family living for Christ? (Not just you but your immediate family)

0——————————————————————————————————————10

3. What specific habits do you do to counter culture as a family or single person?

4. In what ways do you influence your family to be different?

5. Are there areas you wish you were better at living differently than the world?

Read:
____Lev. 10:10(read v.8-9 for context)
____Eph. 5:1-4
____Eph. 5:17-21

6. What discipline(s) sets a believer apart for God? A discipline the world does not know?

7. What discipline(s) do you need help putting into practice and making them a part of your Christian life?

". . distinguish between the holy and the common, between the unclean and the clean."
~Lev. 10:10

In Christ, you are anything but common; you are an heir to the throne, a daughter of the King, royalty, a sister with the power and authority to influence anyone who comes your way! How will you use your influence?

Verses 17-19

8. What is the Lord's promise and reward to the head of this family?

What an honor to never fail to have a man serve God in his family.
What a legacy!
What an influence Jonadab had on his family. Although we don't see his name much in scripture he made a huge impact on God's heart.

Fighter Verse:
Then Jeremiah said to the family of the Rekabites, "This is what the Lord Almighty, the God of Israel, says: 'You have obeyed the command of your forefather Jehonadab and have followed all his instructions and have done everything he ordered.' Therefore this is what the Lord Almighty, the God of Israel, says: 'Jehonadab son of Rekab will never fail to have a descendant to serve me.'" Jer. 35:18-19

Prayer:
Lord, let this be true of my family and me. May I leave a legacy for many generations to come. May the influence I spread be for posterity.

Chapter 36

*For I fully expect and hope that I will never be ashamed, but that I
will continue to be bold for Christ, as I have been in the past. And I
trust that my life will bring honor to Christ, whether I live or die.*
~The apostle Paul
Philippians 1:20 NLT

Verses 1-2

1. Who was on the throne at this time? Refer back to your timeline, what year/time period did this take place?

Verse 3

2. What was God's _hope_ and _plan_ for Jeremiah to write down all that He had revealed to him?

Verse 4

3. Who was in charge of writing the words of Jeremiah?

In this chapter we see how a scribe's skill was used in those days. Without scribes we would probably not have most of God's written word. Baruch was a faithful one, writing down Jeremiah's prophecies twice (as you will see) and not to mention the longest book of the bible!

Verse 5-10

4. Who read the Word and who was there?

Verse 11-19
5. What was the response of the officials?

Verse 20-26
You can't destroy God's Word- it will always find a way.

Can you imagine!?! Having been read the Word of God and then burning the very Words of God? This guy was something else! God's Word cramped his style and he couldn't bear the conviction... or lack thereof and had enough of the ever-present reminder that he was living in sin.

Today, many Asian Christians live without God's Word or very pages from the Bible that have to be passed along from one believer to another because the whole counsel of God- the whole Bible, is forbidden. If caught, Asian Christians could face torture and even death for carrying God's Word around. Although, Christians in this country wouldn't burn their Bibles many of us take God's Word for granted. Many of us don't even open our Bibles. Most of us don't have quiet times and much less have read the Bible in its entirety. We can ignore God's voice in our life simply by not opening the Book and following along. If we want to know God's voice we must know God's Word.

6.   What was the reaction of the king when he heard God's word read from the scroll?

7.   What did the king lack?

Read:
____Proverbs 9:10

8.   How can we gain wisdom and insight?

Read:
____Revelation 22:18-19

9.   What does Jesus tell us not to do in this passage?

10.   What are repercussions of changing God's Word or worse getting rid of it?

Verses 27-32

11.   How did Jeremiah respond to the burning of the scroll?

12.   What inspires you about his actions?

13.   What was Jeremiah's motivation for rewriting words that seemed to fall on deaf ears?

> God's Word brings Hope to our fallen world. Without it we wouldn't
> be able to see Jesus. The Bible is God's breath and a reminder of Jesus. It
> provides everything we need to live the life He has called us to.

14.   Why else is the Bible essential to our walk? Fill in the blanks.

$\mathcal{S}$cripture	$\mathcal{S}$piritual $\mathcal{B}$enefit
Psalm 19:7	
Psalm 119:105	
Psalm 119:111	
John 1:1	
Hebrews 4:12	
What does the Word mean to you?	

Fighter Verse:

"So, Jeremiah took another scroll and gave it to the scribe Baruch son of Neriah, and as Jeremiah dictated, Baruch wrote on it all the words of the scroll that Jehoiakim king of Judah had burned in the fire. And many similar words were added to them." Jeremiah 36:32

Prayer:

Lord, give me the same tenacity that Jeremiah had for your Word. May I not take my Bible for granted, give me discipline to read and study it and the eyes and ears to hear your voice.

Chapter 37

Verses 1-2

1. Who set Zedekiah as king?

2. What nation ruled over Jerusalem at this time?

Verse 3
A Change of Heart?

True change of heart lasts. Fear of circumstances can only control our passion for the Lord so long then when things are back to normal we soon forget out dependence on God.

3. Has there been a time when you clung to God because you needed Him out of urgency then when things returned to normal you became less dependent on Him?

4. How can being less dependent on Him create complacency in your life?

5. What is your dependency on Him like at this moment?

|———————————————————————————————————|

I'm in control!   Hanging on for dear life!

6. Referring to the scale above, if you are in the middle how do you define that level?

7. If you are anything but hanging on for dear life how can you get there? What steps can you take?

Verses 4-8
Putting Hope in the Wrong Place!

Because of fear of the Babylonians and disobedience to God in submitting to Nebuchadnezzar as He had commanded them to do, Zedekiah allied with Egypt for protection against their Babylonian enemy. But as God would have it; Babylon defeated Egypt in 605B.C.

8. What does this reveal about Zedekiah's trust in the Lord?

9. Have you ever put your trust in circumstances rather than God? Have you ever feared your circumstances more than you put your trust in God?

Circle the kind of trust you have:

Flaky   Confident   Depends

Explain:

Answer true or false.

____Do you usually vote for economic stability instead of moral stability?

____Do you start panicking as soon as your financial security starts to slip away and take matters into your own hands before praying for guidance?

____Are you more likely to try fix your problems using any possible method before turning to God?

10. How can you be more like Jeremiah during times of doubt and uncertainty?

Verses 9-20

11. How had Jeremiah's circumstances changed?

12. Did his mission or his response to it change?

13. Have you ever allowed your circumstances to dictate how you respond to God's calling in your life? Have you used them as an excuse not to fulfill His purpose? Explain.

Verse 21
14. How did God choose to protect Jeremiah?

Fighter Verse:

Prayer:

Lord protect me from my enemies. Let me share your gospel. Let me be open to your plan for my life and accept your will. Whatever happens to me help me see your greater purpose.

Chapter 38

Verse 1-5 *The Truth is Bad Propaganda!*

Verses 6-9

1. How does God step in for Jeremiah's safety?

Verse 10

2. How does his reply contrast to his earlier response in verse 5?

3. What does this reveal about the type of King Zedekiah was?

Verse 11-13

4. By interceding for Jeremiah what does this action reveal about Ebed-Melech?

Reread Jeremiah 1:19. How does the promise God made to Jeremiah in chapter 1 ring true in chapter 38:11-13?

Jeremiah could've relaxed in the palace eating bonbons all day in his jammies if he wanted to. He won the mercy of Zedekiah for goodness sake. But he chose the hard road. He saw the opportunity to speak truth; he sought heart change and paid the consequence.

His active life in God reveals that he remained faithful and obedient to God's calling in his older years. He didn't use age as an excuse to not get the job done. In God's economy there is no such thing as retirement. Age is just a number.

Refer back to Jeremiah 1:6. Contrast the time that has gone by in Jeremiah's journey. He started young and is still pursuing his purpose.

5. Do you let age or (in)experience affect how you respond to ministry? Explain.

6. How do you see the length of your calling? How and when do you want it to end?

Verses 14-19

7. Although Zedekiah sought the truth what did he fear the most?

Verse 20-28

Prison is definitely not the outcome you'd expect for someone who has faithfully followed God for the past forty years.

Can you see how God works in our circumstances? He puts us in places where we need to be. His plan is always good even if it doesn't look the way we thought it would. Whether it be in a cistern, a prison, a palace, a bad marriage, a lonely season, a bad work environment, uncertainty, fill in the blank. He's got our back, through thick and thin.

8. What was the hope that carried Jeremiah through is calling?

9. What is the hope that keeps you fulfilling your purpose?

Fighter Verse:

"...Obey the Lord by doing what I tell you. Then it will go well with you, and your life will be spared." Jeremiah 38:20

Prayer:

Lord help me see you in the midst of hardship, duty, the mundane and pain. May I not see you only in comfort- in places that suit me but help me see you in discomfort and places that hurt.

Chapter 39

Verses 1-3

"Now the king of Babylon was very intent and earnest upon the siege of Jerusalem; and he erected towers upon great banks of earth, and from them repelled those that stood upon the walls: he also made a great number of such banks round about the whole city, the height of which was equal to those walls. " "...And this siege they endured for eighteen months, until they were destroyed by the famine, and by the darts which the enemy threw at them from the towers." ~Flavius Josephus
(also see 2 Kings 25:1-4)

Verses 4-7 Lost Hope!

Read:
____2 Kings 24:18-20
____Prov. 14:34

1.   How could Zedekiah have prevented his fate?

Verses 8-10
Notice God's protection over the poor.

Verses 11-14

2.   How does God gain favor for Jeremiah?

Read:
____Daniel 2:25-28

3.   What are the similarities in how God gains favor for Jeremiah and Daniel?

4.   Has the Lord ever gained you favor in a difficult situation? Share your story.

5.   Do you easily recognize the favor of the Lord or do your expectations exceed His blessings? Discuss a time when you didn't see God's blessing clearly at first because you were waiting for something different.

6. Who does God's protection extend to and why?

7. By mentioning these details in scripture what is God revealing about the importance of interceding for and defending those who are doing His work?

Read:
____Prov. 28:26
____Prov. 16:9

8. How important is trusting God in your journey even when it doesn't seem like the logical/popular choice?

Fighter Verse:

"'This is what the Lord Almighty, the God of Israel, says: I am about to fulfill my words against this city—words concerning disaster, not prosperity. At that time they will be fulfilled before your eyes. But I will rescue you on that day, declares the Lord; you will not be given into the hands of those you fear. I will save you; you will not fall by the sword but will escape with your life, because you trust in me, declares the Lord.'" Jeremiah 39:16-18

Prayer:

Lord, in the midst of fear help me trust you. May your presence be ever before me that I see your hand upon me. Make me strong in tough times and give me courage when fear seems to overwhelm me. Let me see hope even before it arrives.

Chapter 40

Verse 1

1. What details are given as to how Jeremiah was taken captive?

Verses 2-3
Isn't it amazing how the enemy knew why war was being waged on God's people! Even he would acknowledge what few of them wanted to.

Verses 4-6

2. What became of Jeremiah after the fall of Jerusalem to Babylon? Where did he wind up?

Verses 7-10
After the deportation to Babylon the poor, weak and few other groups were left behind and Nebuchadnezzar left a Jewish leader in charge of his people. Their new leader was Gedaliah, the son of Ahikim, who saved Jeremiah's life.

Verses 11-12

I3. After observing scripture how was the king of Babylon used to save a remnant for Judah?

Verses 13-16

3. What might have kept Gedadiah from heeding counsel on this matter?

Read:
____Prov. 12:15
____Prov. 11:14
____Prov. 15:22

4. How does God use people in your life as "guideposts?" Explain.

5. Can you remember a time when you were given counsel and you refused to heed it and the consequences were not favorable? Explain.

6. Are there people in your life that counsel you? Do you have people in place that you can go to when you need counsel about a certain issue? Who are they?

If you do not have accountability (guideposts) in your life, can you think of someone that can keep you accountable in your Christian walk. An accountability partner or guidepost is someone who is not afraid to tell you when you're going the wrong direction or off base, she is someone who is faithful to pray for you and with you, she is someone who isn't too busy to ask you how you are doing, she cares about the welfare of you and your family, and she's always read with scripture to encourage you and lift you up. Name a few ladies you might consider asking to be your accountability partner:

Chapter 41

Verses 1-3

1. What was the result of Gedadiah not taking the counsel of his commanders?

Verses 4-5

2. Why were there men coming to the house of the Lord?

Read:
____Leviticus 12:1,12,14

3. What purpose do you think the grain offering had for the Jews?

It is evident that perhaps these men had learned a lesson from the past; the Lord is the giver of all good things.

The irony of this tragedy is that the lesson learned came when they had nothing left. Clarity usually comes when we lose everything. It's poverty, loss, brokenness, need, and want that gives clear perspective. Sometimes He must strip of us of all things before we can truly appreciate all the gifts He bestowed on us in the first place.

Verses 6-15

4. How does this story turn around for the rest of the captives of Ishmael?

5. What becomes of Ishmael?

Verses 16-18

6. Where did Jeremiah, Johanan and the captives end up?

7. Read verse 17, what was driving them to go to Egypt?

8. Have you ever let fear drive you instead of trusting in the Lord?

9. Do you think it was logical for them to go to Egypt?

10. Did God want them in Egypt?

11. Have you made decisions based out of fear? Name them.

12. What were the outcomes?

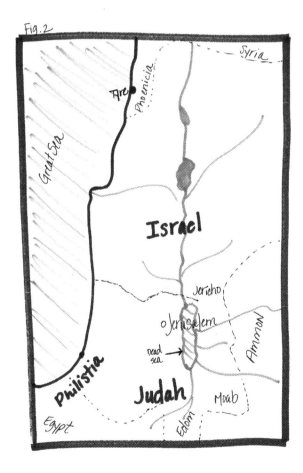

Refer to the map in Fig. 2
Underline Ammon, Moab, and Edom (Present-day Jordon)
Circle Jerusalem.
Cross out Israel (It was no longer a nation after the Assyrian captivity
Draw a line from Jerusalem to Egypt to represent Jeremiah's escape

Edom, Moab, and Ammon are the places where Jews were scattered during the Assyrian exile. Jews continued to escape to these nations to hide from God's judgment.

Although God used one of their enemies (Babylon) to bring judgment and restore a remnant of Judah, there were still enemies at large who wanted to devour little Jerusalem or what was left of her anyway. Although we live in forgiveness we still have an enemy who lives at large. He can only be conquered by the blood of Jesus. He can do no harm that our God does not approve of. He can never have our souls.

Why do you think Israel has always been surrounded by enemies? What profound impact could this little nation have in the midst of many warring giants?

Fighter:
Find a verse about hope and meditate on it and submit it to memory.

Prayer:
Write out your prayer.

Chapter 42

"Make us to choose the harder right instead of the easier wrong and never
to be content with a half-truth when the whole can be won."
~From the Cadet Prayer U.S. Military Academy Chaplain (Col) Clayton Wheat 1919

Verses 1-3 Forgetting a valuable lesson never leads to a favorable outcome.

1. The people ask Jeremiah to pray for what 2 things:

1. _____

2. _____

Read:
____ Jeremiah 36:9-10

2. What had they already learned about God's will?

Fear is a liar.
Fear makes us double-minded, losing perspective and direction. Fear
distorts God's will and makes it appear hazy and unsafe.
If we can remember that God is constant; His plans don't change simply
because our circumstances get rocky, then we can be at peace even things
around us are chaotic. If we can remember that God's plans are always
good then we can rest even when uncertainty looms around us.

Read:

____James 1:5-7

3. How did the Jews relate to the double-minded man in this verse?

Verses 4-6

4. What did the Jews promise Jeremiah when they were to hear the answer from the Lord?

Verses 7-12
The grass is greener where God's mercy is found!

5. What was God's promise if they remained in Babylon?

6. How long did it take God to answer Jeremiah?

7. How do you handle the Lord's delay in answering prayers?

Waiting on God takes discipline. Asking is easier than waiting for a reply. Doing your own thing is faster than waiting to see what He'll say. Waiting, stillness, servitude, quiet, are all essential disciplines in order to hear from the Lord. If we ever want to go in the direction He has for us than we must practice the discipline of waiting. While our culture shouts, "hurry up," "have it instantly," God whispers, "wait," While our schedules demand our feet to run and minds to race, God whispers, "wait." When we fret with concern over unanswered prayers and life's dilemmas, serious and mundane, we ask, "why aren't you answering?" He whispers back, "I did, I said to wait."

8. What did Jeremiah's patience reveal about his discipline in waiting for the Lord's direction?

9. How can you be *different* in waiting on God's reply?

Plant these verses in your life the next time you're finding yourself having to wait on God.

Promises While I Wait	
Isaiah 40:31	Renewed Strength
Psalm 46:10	Healing (hidden meaning)
Psalm 86:7	Answers
Jeremiah 33:3	Revelation

During your quiet time meditate on the lyrics to this song.

"While I'm waiting I will serve You
While I'm waiting I will worship
While I'm waiting I will not faint
I'll be running the race Even while I wait. . .
And I am peaceful. . .
Though it's not easy
But faithfully, I will wait
Yes, I will wait"

Lyrics from While I'm Waiting, John Waller

Verses 13-18
You can run but you can't hide!

10. What were the clear instructions of the Lord?

11. What was the reason they wanted to flee to Egypt (v.14)?

12. What lesson can be learned about trying to flee the discomfort of God's will in our life?

In your own personal life have you ever believed that the grass was/is greener on the opposite side of God's will? Why did the grass seem greener? Was it more convenient to believe that? Explain.

Verses 19-22 *The wrong way always seems right in the beginning but irony strikes when least expected.*

13. What was the fatal mistake the remnant made?

14. If they had taken to heart the experiences during the fall of Jerusalem how might have this experience been different?

15. Can you look back at your journey with the Lord and see the growth and maturity that has taken place? Does obedience come easier than it used to? Explain.

16. What areas in your life would you like to see improve over the next year? Circle those that apply:

Obedience   Faith   Trust   Rest in Him   Confidence   Knowledge of the Word

Discipline   Godliness   Strength against Temptation   Motherhood   Marriage

Calm in my Storm   Loving the Unlovable   Serving Others   _____

Pray over each of these scriptures to be evident in your life.

Read:
____James 1:22
____Colossians 3:12-14
____Ephesians 5:3-4
____1 Peter 1:22

A life verse is a mission statement that defines your life. It reminds us
who we are and what God has done for us. All verses speak life and truth
into us but chose one that especially defines you and your calling.

I have two:

Matthew 6:33
"Seek first the kingdom of God and His righteousness and all these shall be added to you"

(This one reminds me to put God first in all things. It reminds me of His faithfulness in my life when I seek Him first. All things fall into place.)

Jeremiah 20:9
...his word is in my heart like a fire, a fire shut up in my bones.
I am weary of holding it in; indeed, I cannot.

(This one describes the passion I have in my heart to tell others about Him. It reminds me of the day I was saved and that even when I am worn out from the spiritual battle He will continue to burn, in my heart, a passion for His Word.)

If you have a life verse write it out here:

Fighter Verse:

Prayer:
"Sometimes God puts us through the experience and discipline of darkness to teach us to hear and obey Him. Pay attention when God puts you into darkness, and keep your mouth closed while you are there. Are you in the dark right now in your circumstances or in your life with God? Is so, then remain quiet. Darkness is the time to listen. Don't talk to other people about it; don't read books to find out the reason for the darkness; just listen and obey."
~Oswald Chambers

Chapter 43

Verses 1-3

    1. What was the excuse the people gave for not believing Jeremiah's words?

    2. Refer back to Jer. 42:5-6

What did the people promise to Jeremiah upon hearing God's will?

God doesn't always work under the logical realm; faith comes from taking "the road less traveled", believing in His words even when it doesn't make sense. Sometimes it means risking everything to see the plans God has for you.

It wasn't logical for Peter to get out of the boat and attempt to walk on water.
It wasn't logical for Daniel to risk his life for the sake of worshiping a king.
It wasn't logical for Esther to risk her own life for the sake of many others.
It wasn't logical for Abraham to sacrifice his own son.
It wasn't logical for Jesus to die for crimes he didn't commit.

Faith defies logic. Be different. Have faith. Wait on God.

Read:
____Dan. 9:26
____Matt. 24:9-21

    3. Based on these scriptures what does God reveal to us about things to come?

    4. What kind of lady are you, a "stick-it-out" girl or a "take-the-high-road-when-the-going-gets-tough" girl? Is there a pattern in your life that verifies your answer? Explain.

Verses 8-13

    5. What was the result of the people's "arrogant" unbelief

Read:

____1 Peter 4:7-10

____2 Peter 3:10-13, 17&18

6. Write down as many words that describe the way Christians should behave in these times?

7. How do you hope to handle the tough times? Where will your security come from?

God never promises us easy times here on this earth. If we live for Him we can expect that at times the enemy will try and oppress us and at times it may seem like the enemy is winning. In the end though, He promises He will never leave us nor forsake us (Deut. 31:6). He also promises us an eternal reward for sticking it out!

Fighter Verse:

Write out your favorite verse from the study.

Prayer:

Write out your prayer.

Chapter 44

Verse 1

1. Where was Jeremiah? Who was he speaking to?

2. What does this reveal about Jeremiah's determination to speak truth no matter where he was?

Refer back to Jer. 40:4-6

3. Did he want to be in Egypt? Where had Jeremiah chosen to settle?

Verse 2-6
God never leaves us even when we sin. His voice can always be heard; we must discipline ourselves to listen!

Verses 7-8

4. Who does God put the blame on for the consequences they will face?

Verses 9-10

5. How should remembering the sins of previous generations, members in our family help us move forward in our spiritual journey?

Verses 11-14

6. What was the punishment bestowed about the people who disobeyed God? What or who was He going to take away?

Read:
____Ezra 9:12
____Isaiah 10:20
____Romans 11:4&5

7. Based on the scriptures about the remnant what are some qualities that the remnant should possess?

Verses 15-19

8. What was the reason they refused to obey God's words?

9. From whom or what were they drawing their security? (v.18)

Notice, (v.15 and v.19) the emphasis on the husbands awareness of their wife's disobedience and broken fellowship with the Lord. This reveals the lack of protection and accountability within the marriage.

10. Have you given your husband permission to hold you accountable when fellowship with the Lord is broken or when you've slipped away into comfortable complacency?

11. What specific things can you ask your husband to do or say in order to protect you against spiritual complacency?

Read:
____Ecc. 4:9-10

"...A head is given to a woman for protection, safety, and shelter. We must not run from the safety of our own head to what looks like better shelter to us. What a great protection it is to have a head to submit to, rather than being swayed by our own emotions, whims, and fears."
~ Nancy Wilson (From the Fruit of Her Hands)

In order for our husbands to feel comfortable in being our protector in spiritual matters, we must give him permission and freedom to hold us accountable in our walks with the Lord. We must request it- beg for it-by all means give him the whole right to just bring us back when we've gone off the deep end.
If we confuse this for control we miss what God created marriage for.

Read:
____Genesis 3:9-19

12. After disobeying and lying to God in the garden whom did God call on first?

Whom did he call on next? And last?

13. What were their punishments?

Adam:
Eve:
Satan:

In God's economy everyone is held accountable for their own sins, we can't play the blame game. Husbands and wives were designed to partner in spiritual matters- to guard against the enemy and protect their home from evil. Adam and Eve both failed. When we bring temptation and sin into our homes we do the same. We negate the design God gave us. The Hebrew wives didn't protect their homes or their hearts and the husbands didn't hold them accountable.

Verses 20-30 *God will always have the last word!*

Notice in v.24 the inclusion of *all* women.

The men of Jerusalem seem to have a problem with spiritual complacency but a husband's laziness is no excuse for a wife to give into moral depravity or modern-day idols.

14. How do you suppose they could've used their influence in their marriages and homes to do what the right thing? How would this have changed the course of their lives?

    All women were created with influence, whether you are married or not or have children or not. Answer the following regardless of your life stage.

15. How do you use your spiritual influence in your home to encourage, teach, and admonish godly things in your home?

Fighter Verse:
"When the Lord could no longer endure your wicked actions and the detestable things you did, your land became a curse and a desolate waste without inhabitants, as it is today. Because you have burned incense and have sinned against the Lord and have not obeyed him or followed his law or his decrees or his stipulations, this disaster has come upon you, as you now see." Jeremiah 44:22-23

Prayer:
Lord, help me recognize my influence over the people you've placed in my life. Help me own my authority to influence even when I think no one is watching.

Chapter 45

Verse 1
Going back in time

1. Who is Jeremiah speaking to in this passage?

2. Who is king during this time?

Verses 2-3

3. What was Baruch's complaint?

Did you know:

Scribes in ancient times were usually hired by patrons to write and record historical events, data, and the word of God as we see in Jeremiah. They had very comfortable lives financially and were in high demand with most of the population being illiterate. They were considered of high social class and were regarded for their wisdom and intellect. Most, never worried about food, drink or housing. Baruch, the scribe hired by Jeremiah, was not only hired to write the very Words of God down he was present at all of Jeremiah's hardships, trials, and revelations given to him by the Lord. It is likely that Baruch witnessed and endured the same hardships as Jeremiah. Baruch was also a friend and fellow believer in God's Word. In their time together is it easy to imagine Baruch as a disciple of Jeremiah.

Ponder:

The book of Jeremiah gives a rare glimpse into the life of a faithful scribe and the value of their hard work. In this chapter we see the precious relationship between God and scribe. How important are the concerns of man that God would even address them and counsel them? Ponder on this relationship as you answer the following questions.

4. Why do you suppose Baruch was so sorrowful and full of worry?

Verse 4

5. What was God's promise and reminder to Baruch?

Verse 5

6. What was God's 2nd promise?

7. We don't know what "great things" Baruch was searching for but we do see God's response to him.

8. What do Baruch's desires reveal about him?

9. How do you relate to him? Do you share the same struggles?

10. Have you ever taken your eyes off the ministry God has given and put them on the sacrifice you make for Christ in daily life (as a wife, mother, friend, for ministry etc.)?

It is refreshing to know that we are not alone in our struggles of the flesh, that even the godliest men of the bible struggled too. It's also awesome to know that we serve the same God the ancients did. And that He does for us what He did for them! Listens.

Read:
____Phil 4:6
____Matt 6:33
____Col. 3:2

11. How can you apply these verses to your journey?

Fighter Verse: Write your own verse.

Prayer: *Write out your prayer.*

Chapter 46

Verses 1-2
God's jealous love stirs His heart to bring down our greatest idols.

Verses 3-9

1. How does Egypt start their battle?

2. After gearing up what begins to happen?

Verses 10-24

3. How does the battle end for Egypt?

4. What does this reveal about God's pursuit of our love and His willingness to destroy our dependencies on other "gods"?

What does this reveal about forging alliances with God's enemies?

Read:
____2 Corinthians 6:14
____Romans 12:2

5. How did being in Egypt corrupt the people?

Read:
____Exodus 14:12-14

6. After reading this passage how did history repeat itself?

7. What were the Hebrew children afraid of?

Verses 25-26

8. Although punishment is brought on Egypt, what promise is given to her in v.26?

Our idols are God's enemy, when we set our hearts and minds on things other than God we give ourselves over to spiritual warfare. We cannot serve two masters (Matthew 6:24). One thing we can depend on is that God *can* overcome our idolatry if we let Him. He will fight for us! But we must meet him on the battle field!

Verses 27—28
Notice God's undying love for a people who don't deserve it- who continually turn their trust to something false, unreal, mortal, and stone.

9. What was God's hope for the remnant after captivity in Babylon and those left in Jerusalem?

10. Although they missed the mark by a long shot what chance does God give them to have a fresh start?

11. What does this reveal about God's love and hope for His people, His remnant?

12. What image do you have of God based on v.27-28?

   A. A faithful lover chasing and longing after His bride
   B. An angry God waiting expectantly to judge people for their sins
   C. Other _____

13. How has your view or perception of God changed or solidified through the course of this study?

Fighter Verse:
"Do not fear, O Jacob my servant; do not be dismayed, o Israel. I will surely save you out of a distant place, your descendants from the land of their exile. Jacob will again have peace and security, and no one will make him afraid. Jeremiah 46:27

Prayer:
Write out your prayer.

Chapter 47

For you created my inmost being; you knit me together in my mother's womb. I praise you because I am fearfully and wonderfully made; your works are wonderful, I know that full well. My frame was not hidden from you when I was made in the secret place. When I was woven together in the depths of the earth, your eyes saw my unformed body. All the days ordained for me were written in your book before one of them came to be.
~Psalm 139:13-16

Verse 1

1. Who is the object of God's wrath?

Read:
____Gen. 9:18-19
____Gen. 10:6
____Gen. 10:13

Fill in the family tree (according to the scriptures provided):

NOAH
(Patriarch)

Shem	**Ham**	**Japheth**
(son)	(son)	(son)

1._____ 2._____
3._____ 4._____

List out the son's of Mizraim.

2. What relationship did the Philistines have with Noah?

(Circle the son of Noah that was directly related to the Philistines)

3. What heritage did they have with the Lord?

Read:

____Gen. 9:1,7-11

4. What do you observe about their history as God's people?

Verses 2-7 *God always defends His people!*

Read:

____Judges 10:6-7

5. What can we infer from this passage about how the Philistines turned out spiritually?

6. Why is God so angry with the Philistines?

Read:

____Amos 1:6

7. What does this reveal about God's justice for His people and His timing?

Amos prophesized approximately two hundred years before this event took place.

Read:

____Song of Solomon 8:6-7

8. What does this piece of scripture reveal about the type of love God has for us?

9. How does God make His love personal for you? Explain?

10. Do you see God's love for you as passionate and personal?

11. How would you describe the type of love *you* have for Him?

Fighter Verse:

Prayer:
Lord, keep my faith steadfast, my spirit in-step with you, and my heart and mind always on heavenly things; that I may not go astray or grow complacent. May I serve you like Paul and not like the sons and grandsons of Noah?

Chapter 48

Verse 1

    1. Who is the verse concerning?

Read:
____Gen. 19:37

    2. Who was Moab?

    3. What do you observe about Moab's spiritual lineage?

Verses 1-9

    4. Write down as many words that describe Moab's fate?

1.
2.
3.
4.
5.
6.
7.

Verse 6

Bush (NIV) or Juniper (ESV): Hebrew: naked, stripped, and destitute

Verse 7

    5. Why is the Lord angry with the Moabites?

(In what do they put their trust?)

Write out Jeremiah 17:7-8:

    6.   How easy is it to fall into self-reliance in this country?

    7.   What is the danger of depending on wealth, economic security, and our own works?

For by grace you have been saved through faith. And this is not your own doing; it is the gift of God, not a result of works, so that no one may boast. ~ *Ephesians 2:8-9*

> The danger of depending on our own good works is that it can be the very thing that leads us away from God. If we believe we need anything extra than the Cross, then we deceive ourselves into believing God is not enough.

Read:
____2 Cor. 3:5

    8.   What other ways can we fall prey to self-reliance?

    9.   What is the cure for self-reliance?

Verse 10
An enemy of God's people is an enemy of God!

    10. What would be the consequence for anyone not fulfilling his duty in fighting against Moab?

Verses 11-25
God is really angry!

    11. Who was judged in this passage the Israelites or the Moabites?

Read:
____Num. 25:1-3
(For context read all of chapters 22-24)

The history between the Moabites and the Israelites has been one of conflict. God gave Balak several opportunities to bless Israel and all four times Balak became angry and refused. Finally, the Moabite women conquered the souls of the Israelites through sexual immorality. (Num. 25:1&2).

Verses 26-28
Moab becomes a joke!

Verses 29-30

    12. How is Moab described?

Verses 31-36

13. Describe how the Lord feels about the punishment of the Moabites?

14. What does this reveal about God's character?

Verses 37-39
Heads shaved, waists covered in sackcloth, slashed flesh, and mourning, a funeral of a great nation is in procession. A powerful nation has fallen. What a scary time for those who depended on the wealth and security of this once powerful nation. What will the world do if America falls?

***Take this time to pray for America. May we see hearts changed towards Jesus, a culture swayed to goodness and the right to purity.

Verses 40-47

15. What promise does God leave Moab with at the end in v. 47?

Read:
____Amos 2:1-3

God had sent warning to Moab before to turn away from their sin. He warned them with prophetic imagery of harsh things to come. They chose not to heed. Sound familiar in our time?

Let Amos encourage you to spread the gospel, God's love and good news even if it seems like no one is listening.

Fighter Verse:

Prayer:

Chapter 49

1. Who are the Ammonites?

Read:
_____ Gen. 19:35-38

2. What type of moral legacy did they begin with?

Ammon is present-day Jordan

Read:
_____ Deut. 23:3-4

3. Why is God angry with the Ammonites?

Read:
_____ Deut. 2:19

4. Although Ammon had proven to be an enemy to the Israelites how did God chose to let his justice prevail in their lives?

5. What does this reveal about God?

Verses 1-5
Old enemies finally get justice!

> God's justice is God's mercy. If His justice didn't exist hell wouldn't pay for its crimes. His justice is what brings us to our knees in repentance, His mercy is what lifts us up.

Verse 6

6. What did God promise His enemies again?

Verse 7

7. Who are the people of Edom?

Read:
____Gen. 25:30

8. What are the things lacking in Edom that angers the Lord?

Verses 8-10

9. Whose name does God refer to in this passage?

God gets personal with Esau. He doesn't use the name He gave his descendants, Edom; He puts his wrath right on the back of Esau. Do you remember the story of Esau and Jacob, his brother (Gen. 25:29-34)? What lesson can we learn from Esau and the anger now put on him? Selling out doesn't' pay; that is the lesson! Don't sell out your faith, your relationship with God, your obedience and calling for something cheap like culture and convenience. Esau found his birthright worthless and worthless is what he wound up!

Read:
____1 Kings 11:1-8
____Ez. 36:5
___Joe 3:19

10. List other reasons God is angry with Edom?

Verse 11
God really loves orphans and widows!

Verses 12-16

11. What observations do you make about the type of nation Edom was?

Verses 17-18
Evil runs in the family!

God compares Edom with Sodom and Gomorrah who are their relatives.

Verses 19-22
The Lion is gonna get ya!

Read:
____Mal. 1:4-5

12. What promise does God keep against the Edomites? How long?

Remember he restores the land back to Moab and Ammon but to Edom he says he will hate them forever.

13. What hope does this give you that you God is faithful to protect you from your enemies?

Verses 23-27
Insult on injury!

There is always great mourning when a wealthy nations fall. When a powerful nation's economic system collapses there is a negative domino effect that occurs within other nation's economic systems.

Damascus: "silent sackcloth weaver"
Location: Capital of Syria
Sackcloth: course woven fabric worn for mourning or used for bagging
Read:
____Judges 10:6

14. Why is God angry at Syria? Are you starting to see a pattern?

Verses 28-33

15. What will Kedar's and Hazor's fate be?

Read:
____Gen 25:13

Whose hand will God use to bring punishment on them (v.30-31)?

Even God's enemies are His servants!

Read:
____ Jeremiah 27:6

Plug in your president's name here: _____ is God's servant used to bring forth God's will and glory!

Even if you didn't vote for him or like him, Republican or Democrat. God is in control. He works through the circumstances, He is Sovereign. He won't control the human heart but He will work in the circumstances so that His plan can prevail. Our challenge is to trust that it is good even when it doesn't look that way.

Verses 34-39

16. How is Elam's fate similar to Kedar's and Hazor's?

The clans of Elam use to be God's people but their hearts changed from service to God to selfishness. Elam had lines of Levites, priests, and chiefs of tribes. Their ancestry had godly beginnings starting with Shem (Noah's son). But sadly they grew complacent and eventually lost their appetite for godly things.

17. How can complacency lead to turning away from God?

> In reading the Divine assurance of the destruction of all the enemies of the church, the believer sees that the issue of the holy war is not doubtful. It is blessed to recollect, that He who is for us, is more than all against us. And he will subdue the enemies of our souls. ~ Matthew Henry

Fighter Verse:
Find a verse that helped you get through the week.

Prayer:
Help me remember your sovereignty no matter who is in power. Nothing on earth is a surprise to you and my faith shall not waver because of political animosity or strife nor shall it rest at the sight of {superficial} political calm. Only in you do I trust.

Chapter 50

Verses 1-2
No Enemy goes unpunished!

Verse 3
Hope is lost; a legacy dies.

Verses 4-7

1. What is the final fate of Israel as the Lord declares?

Read:
___Psalm 126:1-6

2. What promises does God make to his people here?

Read:
___Isaiah 44:6-8
___Isaiah 44:24-28

3. What claims does God make about Himself in this passage?

4. What should our response be to these truths?

Verses 8-18
God is our defender!

Verses 19-20

5. What promise does God make about forgiving Israel and Judah from their sin?

O Israel, put your hope in the Lord, for with the Lord is unfailing love and with him is full redemption. He himself will redeem Israel from all their sins. ~ Psalm 130:7-8

Although God's people have shamed themselves, disobeyed God,
turned away from Him and ultimately rejected the love He had
for them He still pursues them with an everlasting love.

Read:
____Psalm 103:12-13

6. How has God's love for you been evident in your life?

7. Have you reciprocated His love? How? In what ways?

Verses 21-33
When the Tables Turn!

As you read through the punishment God has set for Babylon it seems ironic that he also used them to bring punishment on his own people. Babylon never saw it coming.

Verse 34
Redeemer: (ga'al) Hebrew.: to redeem, avenge, do the part of a kinsman.

A redeemer restores rights to others who have lost them. God calls Himself our redeemer.

Frequently people will say that the God of the Old Testament is quite different than the God of the New Testament but He's never said anything different about Himself. He's remained constant throughout scripture. Through the long journey from complacency to bondage to a nation set on hope of redemption; God has remained a faithful warrior, pursuer, and redeemer of His people. His beloveds didn't deserve their rights but God fought relentlessly to give make sure they had them forever. This is why He sent Jesus.

The Lord your God is with you, the Mighty Warrior who saves. He will take great delight in you; in his love he will no longer rebuke you, but will rejoice over you with singing. Zephaniah 3:17

Verses 35-40

8. What weapons does God command against Babylon?

9. What is the result of the devastation (v.39&40)?

Verses 41-46
Pride Before a Fall

Did you know:

During the times of Babylonian rule there were 3 major Middle Eastern world powers: Persia (Iran) who allied with the Medes, Egypt, and Babylon (Iraq).

[2]Babylon's splendor was built on commerce by the produce of farmers and merchants and protected by a vast military of Chaldeans. The enormous city was built on the back of slaves who were captives of war. Part of the Babylonian slave groups was the Judeans. They endured harsh, abusive treatment and even death. The enclosed city was the approximate size of Chicago. Stones that surrounded the walled city were found to have the inscription, "I am Nebuchadnezzar, King of Babylon."

Talk about a prideful king. They were the strongest nation of their times. They conquered Assyria and later Egypt. Alters surrounded the city gates so the people could worship as they walked past. This was the culture that ensnared the Israelites in the past. Now they were in deep with idol worship with nowhere to escape. Although the reign of the Babylonians was short the iron fist of Nebuchadnezzar reached far and wide conquering Assyria, Egypt, and Judah.

The bigger they are the harder they fall. God used Persia under King Cyrus to defeat Babylon and it never again regained its splendor as in the past.

10. How does this historical event give credibility to the bible?

11. How does God's promise of Babylonian destruction affirm the promises to his people in Isaiah 29:5?

12. What does this reveal about how fast an enemy nation falls?

Many economists predict the fall of America in the near future. There are many analysts who give various credible reasons for America's decline. Regardless of any logical explanation God is in charge. As we've observed in scripture through the book of Jeremiah as soon as a nation strays from loving God it falls. The lack of morality ranks high in the reason for the decline of all nations. Even though immorality ruins nations God still uses all nations for His purpose.

Ponder:
A group called The Adventurers who sought fortune and land in a new world established America first in 1607. As the knowledge of this new world spread to Europe, Separatists of England, came to seek spiritual refuge from King James. They are known as the Pilgrims. They weaved our nation with a spiritual fabric and introduced this land to Christianity. That was only four hundred years ago. Where do you see America heading?

---

[2] Streams of Civilization, Vol. 1, Mary Stanton & Albert Hyma pg. 100-103

13. What is your calling as a Christian in this nation?

14. What similarities and differences does America have to Babylon and to Israel?

15. What noticeable differences in morality have you noticed in American since you were a child?

16. How do these compare to a Biblical worldview?

A Biblical Worldview is a core outlook on life that measures all things against the lenses of the Bible. A question a Biblical Worldview person might ask when deciding on a belief is, "What does God think about this?" Or, "How did Jesus teach on this subject?"

Everyone has core beliefs and worldviews. We need to decide which one we have and if it lines up with God's view. At the end of this life that is what's going to matter.

17. What specific things can you do with your spiritual gifts to bring your generation closer to Jesus.

Fighter Verse:
"Announce and proclaim among the nations,
lift up a banner and proclaim it;
keep nothing back, but say,
'Babylon will be captured;
Bel will be put to shame,
Marduk filled with terror.
Her images will be put to shame
and her idols filled with terror.' Jeremiah 50:2

Prayer:
Thank you, Jesus, for being my great defender, protector and healer.

Chapter 51

Verse 1 *God's vengeance is still raging against Babylon!*

Spirit (NIV, ESV): Anger

Verses 2-4

    1. How will Babylon fall?

Verse 5

    2. What reason does God give for destroying Babylon?

Read:
____2 Kings 25:8-10
____2 Kings 25:16-21

    3. What vengeance was God seeking for his people?

Verses 6-10

Historically Babylon fell and never recovered her great blow from the Lord. This passage reveals that God's truths are evident in history. No matter how much some may refute the Bible as true its historical passages have been proven as true accounts.

Read:
____Micah 7:8-10

    4. What is the promise God gives his people against his enemy?

Verses 11-13

    5. Who does God use to bring justice to Babylon?

Medes: Persia

Did you know:

Geographically Babylon was located next to the Euphrates and prospered due to the proximity to the water. Commerce grew because of trade via sea fare. Many depended on the wealth and health of this world power. Waters are often a metaphor for satisfaction, refreshing, thirst quenched, and success.

Many see America in this way. We are a healthy and wealthy nation (so far), we prosper because of commerce and other nations depend on our political stability.

Read:

____John 4:14

6. What does God promise of His water?

7. What water do you depend on? The Eternal Spring? Or the financial spring of this country?

8. It is easy to fret when our nation's finances are in trouble but where is God asking us to put our trust?

Verses 14-19

God's Power v.15, 16 &19	Babylon's Power v.17-18
1. He made the earth	Senseless with out knowledge
2.	Shamed by idols
3.	Fraud
4.	Worthless objects
5.	Will perish
6.	
7.	
8.	

Pray and meditate over God's power from the list above.

Verses 20-23

God addresses King Cyrus of Persia- he names him and commands him in this verse.

King Cyrus (Cyrus the Great): King of Persia (present-day Iran) 559-530 BC

9. How will God use him?

10. How does this historical document give scripture relevance and credibility?

11. What does this reveal about the power has over other nations?

12. How secure do you feel knowing that God controls even our enemies?

Verses 25-26

13. What guarantee does God make about Babylon?

Verses 27-32

14. According to scripture how did God use the Medes and Cyrus to win the war against Babylon?

Verses 33-48
God's not done!

Threshing floor: an analogy to be broken down like corn on a threshing floor.

Verses 49-51

Like the Greeks the Babylonians had many gods. These gods were introduced to the Israelites and soon their practices and deities were adopted into the Jewish faith.

15. According to this passage does God allow all "inclusive" worship of other gods?

16. Can you be a Christian and believe and practice other religions?

17. How does God's culture differ from our culture in this regards?

Read:
____2 Kings 17:7-8, 18
____John 14:6

18. How would you explain this truth to a nonbeliever who believes that God doesn't mind if we believe in other religions and ideologies contrary to the bible?

Verses 52-53

19. What is the consequence of idol worship for Babylon?

20. What is God's purpose in this?

Verses 54-58

21. What does this reveal about God's vengeance?

Read:
____Romans 12:19

22. Are we justified to get vengeance on someone when they hurt us?

Read:
____Psalm 94:1-6

23. Why does God take vengeance?

Remember: that the Babylonians introduced a god that required child sacrifices, sacrifices of living children, newborns, infants, children. A gift our God gave as a blessing they threw into the fire. Could anyone stop such atrocities so commonly accepted at that time? Only a mighty God could stop it.

God's vengeance is God's way of defending his beloved, the weak, the poor, the fatherless and orphans- His creation.

24. How do you feel knowing you have a mighty defender on your side? There isn't any evil that can harm you that will not be repaid by your Heavenly Father.

The nature of God cannot tolerate abuse or violence. We may not see the day of vengeance or retribution but know that God works in timing, in the invisible and He's always thinking about us.

Verses 59-64
The end of the road!

When Jeremiah started his journey he began warning, speaking truth, interceding, and pleading with and for his own people, the Israelites. Now the tables have turned, the prophetic message is now against the very people that God used to discipline his own people.

25. Who was king of Judah at this time?

26. What year of his reign was this scroll delivered?

In approximately 594/593 BC this message was delivered to Babylon. Eight years later Babylon ceased to be a nation- forever.

Fighter Verse:
"He who is the Portion of Jacob is not like these, for he is the Maker of all things, including the people of his inheritance-the Lord Almighty is his name." Jeremiah 51:19

Prayer:
Lord, help me understand your ways, help me grow in my love for you. Give me faith that surpasses my doubt and questions. Answer when I call on you. Reveal yourself to me. Help me love others to you. Amen!

Chapter 52

Verses 1-30
Jerusalem's last day!

God is patient but he doesn't wait forever.

Jerusalem Finally falls. God gave Jerusalem 136 years after Israel was captured by the Assyrians to turn from their ways, to acknowledge him, repent of their sin and return to him. They refused. In 586 BC the last remaining physical remnant of God's Holy land was burnt, destroyed, robbed and turned over to Babylon, no longer to be a whole nation again until May 14, 1948- as prophesized in Ezekiel 37:11-14.

Verse 31
God keeps his promises at all costs!

Why would God keep an evil man alive after all others have died?

1 Kings 9:5
'then I will establish your royal throne over Israel forever, as I promised David your father, saying, 'You shall not lack a man on the throne of Israel.'

God promised King David that he would always rule over Israel, theoretically he couldn't always rule because he would one day die. But this passage meant that his lineage would always sit on the throne and he kept Jehoiachin alive for that reason. Jesus came from the lineage of King David and had Jehoiachin died the lineage would have died with him.

God turns bad into good. He brings good things from bad things. He redeems. He gives us an example of redemption through his own family line. There are murderers, adulterers, prostitutes, thieves, and idolaters in the same lineage as Jesus and yet he shows us that there is forgiveness at the Cross and that every stronghold in our life can be broken through the blood of Jesus.

After reading the book of Jeremiah we discover why God can't just let things go. He loves us!

God loves us so much that he pleads with us to turn from our
sin because he doesn't want us to stay that way.

He wants us to live a full life in him (John 10:10). He is not a forceful God so he won't push us into loving Him; he patiently waits until we are exhausted of doing things our own way. He loves us so much he sent Jesus to prove it.

So, what do we owe to a God who laid out the heavens, created the earth, moves mountains, walked on water, turns water to wine and yet has the capacity to walk in dirty sandals, touch lepers, forgive prostitutes, make simple fishermen his closet friends and the heart to love them all. Love. We owe him our love.

And how do we love a God that has it all?
What does loving your God with all your heart mind and soul look like?
First things first, you can't love a God you do not know. Reading your bible daily is essential to getting to know your Father. Here are other ways you can demonstrate your love for Him:

-------------------------Living to love God-------------------------

1. **Give your heart to him**. He won't settle for half of you or simple works.

Today I give my life to you:_____

Date:

Today I rededicate my life to you:_____

Date:

2. **Walk in the purpose He created for you**. Write out a purpose statement:

I am born to:_____

_____

3. **Break free from complacency.** Make a commitment to become a student of God's Word. Grow in the grace and knowledge of our Lord Jesus Christ.

Make a commitment statement.
I commit to reading your Word daily. I commit to praying daily.

Signature:_____

Date:_____

Witness:_____
(Have a prayer partner or accountability partner sign with you)

4. **Rewrite and live out your life verse:**

(Write it out here):

5. **Don't hide your faith!**

Read:

___John 21:13-15

Before Jesus' crucifixion Peter denied knowing Him three times. When Jesus returned after His resurrection He surprised the disciples at the same place where they're calling started, the beach, by a fire pit, the same place Peter denied Jesus. Why there, why at that time? Because that is the place it all started. They started their journey not knowing Jesus, sometimes doubting Him, sometimes unsure of His words. He came to confirm their calling, to send them out into the world to radically change it.

Jesus gives them another calling this time. The first one was to follow now He's asking them to lead. They've learned His ways; they were taught well, now they're ready for the mission.

Jesus directly asks Peter a simple question, "Do you love me?" How sweet those words. I can imagine the immense regret Peter had in his heart for his cowardly responses before Jesus was arrested. Oh! the pain he must've endured thinking about it, the sleepless nights he must've repented over it. His purpose? To redeem Peter and confirm His calling. Peter was called from the beginning, no denial was going to come between that.

Now Jesus presses Peter for the one thing that he was made to- the thing he'd been training for all along- to be a shepherd. To care for his people, to teach them, to protect them, to love them, to disciple them.

He challenges Peter with an urgent command, "feed my sheep."

The work is not done: there are people who do not know Jesus, a culture who desperately needs truth, dark places of this world that light, wounds that need healing, and slaves that need freeing.

Jesus is asking Peter to show his love by feeding his sheep. So, what is the thing you can give to a God that has it all- your love. Give to Him what you were born to give-love.

Love God, love others,

"Therefore, go and make disciples of all nations, baptizing them in the name of the Father and of the Son and of the Holy Spirit, and teaching them to obey everything I have commanded you. And surely, I am with you always, to the very end of the age." Matt. 28:19-20

Today, I commit to the great commission as an expression of my love for Jesus, the one who came who gave it all for me.

I will accept opportunities presented to me as a means to share Christ. I will ask the Holy Spirit to empower when such circumstances arise.

I will submit to prayer all those in my life who need Jesus live selflessly so that others can see Christ in me. In Jesus name Amen!

Signature:_____

Date:_____

About the Author

Sara Estevez holds a Bachelors in Business Administration with a concentration in International Business from the University of Texas at San Antonio.

Sara is an active member of Officer Christian Fellowship and Bible study teacher to the Coast Guard Academy as well as a curriculum writer. She created Simple Truths Ministries with the purpose of sharing the Bible's simple truths about Jesus Christ with military cadets and women at her local church. Her passion is to help people fall in love with Jesus by helping them understand how to study the Bible more thoroughly.

Sara is a homeschool mom to three children and a step-mama to a beautiful step-daughter who just received Jesus as her Lord and Savior at Emory University. She is blessed to call Carlos her husband and together they live in Southeast Connecticut.

Printed in the United States
By Bookmasters